CONTENTS

INTRODUCTION

This is a book which looks at the traditional ceremonies and customs which are still carried out in London today, and some of the people involved in them, particularly the costumes they wear.

London traditions span the range from the grandest ceremony still to be seen (but alas not very frequently), the Coronation, to the more recent festivities brought to London by new arrivals – such as the Notting Hill Carnival and the Lion dances of the Chinese New Year.

Many of London's traditions are associated with its most ancient part, the City of London, so it seems appropriate to have a separate chapter on its history and growth.

Tradition has always played an important and useful part in City life. It was for example vital to hold a simple ceremonial to mark the parish boundaries, so that everyone knew exactly where they could either till the ground or build a house. The ceremony of the keys was not just a simple business of locking doors to keep marauders outside, it was a well conceived drill that ensured the safety of the person who locked the gates.

City ceremonial called for groups of people to walk in procession – again this was not just a matter of ceremony, but one of safety in numbers. The equivalent of today's muggers were much more prevalent in the main streets of London in the past. It was no accident that the king preferred to go by boat to the Tower than to ride through the streets – which were not very clean anyway. Hence the sweet smelling nosegays carried by gentlemen in processions, a foil for the foul smells of the gutter, also supposedly a protection against the plague. Merchants of the past having made large sums of money, or in some cases, miraculously survived a danger, would donate to charity and then make sure that their memory lived on in a commemorative service. Many of these survive, instituted by worthy people from all walks of life, otherwise forgotten.

Westminster established its own traditions based on royal connections including the State Opening of Parliament – an annual spectacle which involves searching the cellars of the Palace of Westminster the night before, an acknowledgment of Guy Fawkes' plot but unfortunately quite as necessary today.

The Trooping the Colour combines military splendour with royal ceremony involving all members of the royal family, watching or participating. It is one of the few military traditions or ceremonials carried out in public in London. The Changing the Guard is another, although it seems more of a ceremonial than a mounting of the guard of the sovereign. Trafalgar Day is one ceremony which marks a military victory while the Cenotaph ceremony is a tribute to those who gave their lives in two world wars.

The presence of the River Thames was essential to life in London in the past; and ceremonies which mark the skill of the boatsmen survive, as does the marking of the swans, although this now takes place up-river. The Oxford/Cambridge Boat Race is as much a celebration of the coming of spring as a test of skills.

London's former villages which are today's suburbs and prosperous commercial centres continue in many ways the traditional annual fairs and markets of the past. In some cases they even recall their rural past as in the

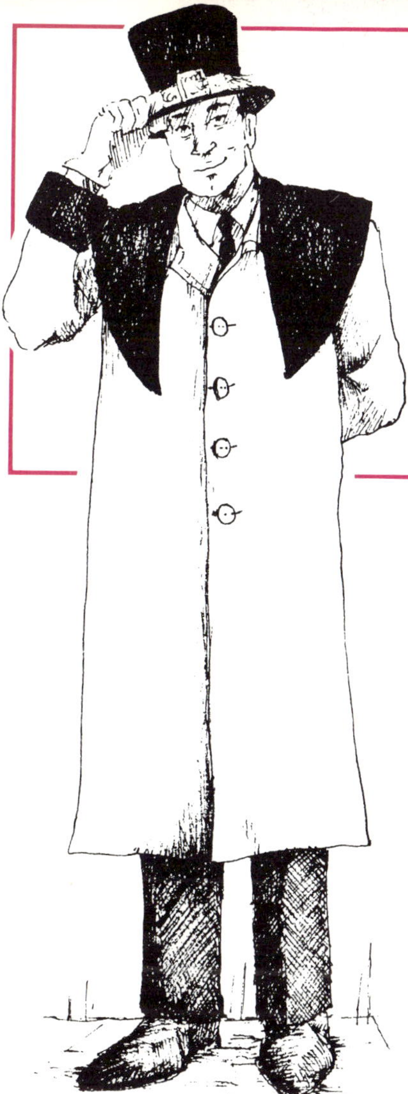

LONDON'S DOORMEN

The doormen of London's institutions and grand hotels are of imposing stature and elegance; they also have a great deal more power and influence than is apparent to the casual visitor. This is the Head Doorman at Lloyd's of London now on duty at the glittering glass and tubular steel edifice created by Richard Rodgers and Partners but still dressed in his red coat and top hat. He is assisted by "waiters" who work inside the building and take their name and livery in recognition of Lloyd's modest beginnings as a coffee house.

BRIDGEMASTER

The Bridgemaster and his staff of attendants at Tower Bridge only recently acquired their uniform when the Bridge opened to the public in 1982. It is modelled on that worn by naval officers at the turn of the century and the cap is a compromise between a naval and a civilian peaked cap. The Bridgemaster wears a white stiff, fly-away collar, black tunic jacket with gold bands on the sleeve, denoting his seniority, and matching trousers.

Lambeth Country Show – very much in an urban setting. At Southall the only remaining horsemarket continues and the working horse still survives on the streets of London.

London's costermongers are represented by the Pearly Kings and Queens in this book but the rich tradition of street-cries and itinerant street vendors survives in many of London's street markets albeit in a changed and sometimes refined form.

Amongst the changes are "the new images" of London – gone, almost, is the bowler-hatted gent with his rolled umbrella and in his stead, we have the colourful punk who after more than ten years shows no sign of disappearing and therefore deserves a place in this book. Also here to stay are the ceremonies and traditions of the groups of immigrants from many different countries who have made a home in London; Jewish, Greek and Italian – they have all made a mark, followed by West Indians, Indians and Pakistanis, people from Bangladesh and in several bursts people from Hong Kong and most recently Vietnam. It is a credit to London that in due course their festivities such as the Notting Hill Carnival and Chinese New Year become part of the traditional calendar to be enjoyed by all.

PUNKS

"Punks" started to appear in London in the '70's wearing striking clothing mostly a combination of black, tartan, chains and safety pins with elaborate hair-styles in bright colours.*

The movement gained impetus with the arrival of the Sex Pistols pop group in 1976 and a shop established in Kings Road Chelsea which catered for their taste in black leather. Punk music is no longer a force in pop music but the fashion continues and punks, generally non-belligerent and friendly, have become part of the London scene – to be seen in Kings Road, Trafalgar Square and other places.
**"Punk" was an 18th century term for a young ruffian.*

THE HISTORY OF THE CITY OF LONDON

The foundations of the City of London's importance were laid out more than 19 centuries ago at the time of the Roman invasion of A.D. 43. The Romans built a bridge across the Thames and made Londinium, as they named it, the centre of their road system and the seat of their financial officials, protecting it with strong walls.

Londinium, with its river and road connections, attracted trade and there is no doubt the earliest municipal form of administration flourished in London under the Romans. Fragments of their wall can still be identified, so can the imprint of Roman institutions be seen in the modern government of the City.

In the first century of the Roman occupation Tacitus described the City of London as a "town of the highest repute and a busy emporium for trade and traders". In those days the Roman Wall of London enclosed only 325 acres but later during the Saxon period a girdle of land beyond the wall was attached and the present City area of 677 acres was constituted.

The City of London emerged from the Saxon period no less important. Alfred the Great appointed his son-in-law in the year 886 to be its governor and Middlesex was soon subordinated to London. After the Norman Conquest, William the First, by charter of 1067, confirmed the rights and privileges formerly enjoyed by the citizens under Edward the Confessor. The commercial importance of London and the privileges acquired by royal charters naturally gave rise to a sense of corporate responsibility and unity.

London's path to becoming a capital City was set by William the Conqueror, forever known in the City as William the Norman, in reverence to his message to the people of London which promised to observe the laws of Edward the Confessor.

The City has no charter of incorporation for it acted as a unified community in law before the theory of incorporation was evolved. This unification into a commune or corporation, had royal sanction or confirmation in 1191 and led to the appointment of a mayor as head of the community.

The duties of London's administration rested originally with the aldermen each within his own ward. For common action, the aldermen met in a court of aldermen at which the mayor presided. It was this court which in the 13th century,summoned commoners from the wards to give assistance and advice and so made provision for the future Council, which soon came to be appointed by ward elections. By 1346, an authority of mayor, aldermen and councilmen was established.

Like the constitution of Britain, the constitution of the City Corporation is largely unwritten. Its right of amendment was granted by a charter of 1377. It is under these provisions that the Common Council regulates the election of Lord Mayor, Sheriffs and Common Councilmen.

Today the Lord Mayor holds office for only one year but in earlier times mayors frequently held office for considerable periods. A 14th century mayor was elected four times and the legendary Dick Whittington, usually credited with three mayoralties, was elected three times but was mayor four times. Although Whittington was an extremely generous man, he was never knighted but there is an early engraving of him holding a cat so at

LORD MAYOR OF THE CITY OF LONDON

The Lord Mayor's dress varies with the functions he has to attend. Everyday wear in Mansion House where he receives guests, is morning suit and the heavily jewelled badge of office which has been worn by the Lord Mayor since the 16th century. For attendance at City Corporation meetings of the Court of Common Council, he wears a violet gown trimmed with bear fur, a lace jabot (an ornamental frill at the shirt front), knee breeches, black stockings and buckled shoes. For royal occasions he wears a gown of black satin with gold braid (shown here) and for official receptions he wears a scarlet gown trimmed with sable. On certain ceremonial occasions, elections for example, he carries a posy of flowers.

least that part of the legend could be true.

During the 16th century, the City's Court of Common Council developed a reputation for outspokeness, particularly against the monarch. This came to a height over George III's policy towards the American colonies particularly in respect of the new taxation laws. One man who was incensed by the unfairness of George III's decree and sensed not only the forthcoming agitation which would lead to war, but the danger of an entire separation, was John Wilkes, the Mayor in 1774. Wilkes had a fearful reputation. He was made an alderman while a prisoner in the Tower and was said to be one of the ugliest men in London. Yet he had an irresistible charm and was also a member of the infamous Hellfire Club. But he spent his life-time fighting for the freedom of the press and the individual.

London had changed dramatically in the 100 years before Wilkes came to office. The Great Fire of 1666 almost razed the City to the ground. Samuel Pepys recalled in his diary how he went to see the King who commanded him to tell the Lord Mayor to pull down houses and form a safety barrier between the conflagration and what remained of the City.

It was out of the old disease-ridden square mile with its squalid streets and filthy alley-ways that much of what today is so carefully preserved, was created. But the City of Wren, which first emerged and then became entwined with the trading needs of the 18th century and in turn overshadowed by the dominance of the banks, was to be devastated once again. This time it was not by one fire, but a series of fires which were to strike again and again during the Second World War.

Once more London was rebuilt and from the ashes rose buildings which were to make the City a leader in the world's financial markets and through the Barbican Centre, built almost within the fringe of the original Roman Wall, a major contributor to the nation's cultural wealth.

The City is still changing, while maintaining many of the traditions which have been evolved over 800 years of civil history. The needs of London's own financial institutions and those of the world are dictating a new shape to the City of London. A shape governed by international communications in which the city never sleeps and thinks in yen as much as in dollars and sterling.

This new City of chromium and steel where buildings created by Wren and Seiffert sit side by side, justifiably earns the title of "unique" among world cities.

BURLINGTON BEADLES

The Burlington Beadles are in charge of enforcing the special rules of the Burlington Arcade, situated off Piccadilly and built in 1819 on the side of Burlington House. These include no singing, no carrying of open umbrellas and no running. At one time they were all ex-soldiers of the 10th Hussars and they are still ex-servicemen. Their livery has hardly changed since 1819 – a grey frock coat with gold rings on the sleeves, a grey top hat with a gold band and gold trim and a cape in bad weather.

FLOWER GIRLS

"Buy a Flower, Sir" was the cry heard from the Royal Exchange, to Covent Garden and later Piccadilly Circus from the Flower Girls of London selling posies and buttonholes to gentlemen. "Buy my Sweet Roses!" said Eliza to Professor Higgins as she met him outside St. Paul's Church, Covent Garden after a night at the Opera. Covent Garden still sees the occasional "flower girl" dressed in 19th century style for a special event and there are stalls selling wonderful selections of flowers – but the real flower girls are a thing of the past.

Alphabetical list of traditions and ceremonies
(Dates see p.58)

THE BADDELEY CAKE

On Twelfth Night, an 18th century custom is still observed at the Theatre Royal, Drury Lane. The cast, in full costume, and staff join immediately after the performance, in private, to cut the Baddeley Cake, which takes its name from Robert Baddeley once a pastry cook, who became an actor. He died shortly after falling ill dressing for his part in Sheridan's School for Scandal. In his will he left £100 to provide for a Twelfth Night cake at the theatre. Twelfth Night used to be celebrated and cakes were customarily eaten on this night, but nowadays Twelfth Night passes virtually unnoticed, apart from this theatrical occasion, and Epiphany sermons. (See p. 25)

This is a private ceremony, not open to the public.

BEATING THE BOUNDS

The tradition of Beating the Bounds, when choirboys and parishioners walk in procession around the parish boundaries, is still continued among several London parishes on Ascension Day. The Romans had a God of boundaries called Terminus, in whose honour they used to walk in procession around their fields making sacrifices for the protection of their crops. The Christian version is the Beating of the Bounds. One of the most colourful of these processions takes place every three years and starts from the Tower of London at the Chapel Royal of St. Peter ad Vincula. The Chief Yeoman Warder of the Tower, dressed in his state uniform with its long red coat, leads the choirboys around the 31 parish boundary marks in the surrounding streets. One of the marks is in the middle of the main road and traffic is stopped while the chaplain recites a prayer and the choirboys beat the mark vigorously with willow wands. This part of the ritual was to show the population, which was mainly illiterate, exactly where the parish boundaries lay and impress it upon their minds.

The service at the Chapel Royal starts at approximately 1800 hrs (check the time nearer the date).

Members of the public are welcome to join the procession but must leave when it returns to the Tower.

A procession also takes place on Ascension Day each year at All Hallows by the Tower, EC3 at 1500 hrs and has one particularly interesting feature – as the parish marks include one in mid-Thames, a Port of London vessel conveys those officiating from Tower Pier to mid-stream where a boy is held by the ankles as he 'whacks' the boundary over the edge of the boat! When the Tower of London ceremony coincides, it includes a confrontation between the two processions at an historic disputed boundary mark on Tower Hill, and on some occasions the Lord Mayor of London himself comes to challenge the Governor of the Tower.

The public are welcome to join the procession (no charge).

BEATING RETREAT

Beating Retreat is a popular military display of marching and drilling bands of the Household Division and is second only to Trooping the Colour as a parade of Service pageantry and precision. Performed on Horse Guards Parade in late May or early June, it provides a grand display by mounted bands, trumpeters, massed bands and pipe and drums. Some of the performances are given later in the evening by floodlight, and tiers of seats are erected around Horse Guards Parade.

Tickets are available from the end of February on application to Premier Box Office, 1b Bridge Street, SW1. Tel: 01-839 6815/836 4114.

Beating or Sounding Retreat is a similar massed band display, also on Horse Guards Parade, performed by a different Division each year. The title of the ceremony has nothing to do with the defeat or retreat from the field of battle. It is the retreat of sunlight and the onset of night that is signalled or 'beaten', as was the custom long ago. It takes place a few days after the Household Division's Beating Retreat.

Ticket arrangements as above.

BLESSING THE THROATS

The 13th century crypt of St. Etheldreda's Roman Catholic Church, Ely Place, EC1, welcomes pilgrims for the Blessing of the Throats on the feast day of St. Blaise, 3 February. The service is specially designed for all who suffer from diseases or ailments of the throat. At regular intervals of about 15 minutes, the priest comes to the crypt to administer the blessing. Carrying two consecrated unlit candles, which he places in the form of a cross, the priest holds them against the throat of each person. He then pronounces the blessing of St. Blaise, who was martyred in AD316 during the Christian persecution. Legend has it that he performed a miraculous cure of a boy who was about to die because a fish bone had stuck in his throat. Later, in prison, prior to his martyrdom, a woman came to his cell with a gift of candles, whereupon St. Blaise said all who made a similar offering in future would have his protection. The church is a survivor of the days when the town residence of the Bishop of Ely was in the present Hatton Garden area and was the first pre-Reformation church to be regained by the Roman Catholics in London.

Public welcome to attend.

BOAR'S HEAD PRESENTATION

In a ceremony which dates from the 12th century, the Lord Mayor of London is presented with a Boar's Head on a Butcher's Stretcher every December (usually the second Wednesday), by the Worshipful Company of Butchers. In 1343 the City granted the butchers a piece of land in Seacoal Lane adjoining what was then the Fleet River where they could clean "the entrails of beasts". In return they were to give the Lord Mayor a Boar's Head. The butchers only held the land for a few years but a tradition had been established and continues to the present time.

The ceremony is not open to the public although visitors may watch the procession as it leaves Butchers Hall, 87 Bartholomew Close, EC1 for

Mansion House, travelling via Little Britain, St. Martin Le Grand and Cheapside. Check with LTB nearer the date for timings.

BOAT RACE

Oxford University and Cambridge University first raced each other from Hambledon Lock to Henley in 1829. The present 4¼ mile course from University Stone, Putney to Mortlake was first used in 1845 and the race became an annual event in 1856.

This fiercely competitive race is rowed between the two rival teams of the Universities on a Saturday in March or April. The starting time for the race varies, according to tides and the fastest time for the course so far is 16 minutes 45 seconds, set by Oxford in 1984. The second crews for each University (Isis for Oxford and Goldie for Cambridge) also race, approximately 30 minutes before the main race.

Excellent views of the race can be had from The Dove Inn, 19 Upper Mall, Hammersmith, W6 and The Ship Inn, Ship Lane, Mortlake, SW14.

Check with LTB on 01-730 3488 for exact date.

BRIDEWELL SERVICE

Held on the second Tuesday in March at 1200 hrs this annual service of dedication and thanksgiving in St. Bride's Church in Fleet Street commemorates the foundation of Bridewell Royal Hospital by Edward VI on 26 June 1553. The Lord Mayor, dressed in his state robes, attends the service which relates the achievement of Edward VI who, spurred by an evocative service by Bishop Nicholas Ridley (a Bishop at the time of the Reformation and later a Protestant martyr) established a reformatory and school as a home for the poor in the Royal Palace of Bridewell. Unfortunately the realisation turned sour. The hospital became a workhouse in which the inmates suffered extreme hardships from overwork and miserable conditions. The "hospital" in Blackfriars became part prison and only part school. One of its features was a public whipping post which attracted spectators to watch punishments meted out to the inmates. It was rebuilt after the Great Fire of 1666 and became more of a place of learning. It is now a co-educational school known as King Edward VI's School, Witley, nr. Godalming, Surrey.

Public welcome to attend.

BUBBLE SERMON

Richard Johnson was a member and benefactor of the Stationers' Company in 1785 and, when he died in January 1795, he left money for the poor of the company and to provide for an annual sermon on the subject, of "Bulla est vita humana", which had to be without variation. Each year on the first Tuesday in June, members of the company gather to honour their benefactor and listen to the sermon, which translated is "Life is a Bubble". The service is held in St. Martin's-within-Ludgate, EC4 at 1045 hrs to which members of the Stationers' Company walk in procession, leaving Stationers' Hall at 1035 hrs.

Public welcome to attend.

BUTTERWORTH CHARITY

This originated from the custom of placing 21 new sixpences upon a grave in the churchyard of St. Bartholomew the Great, Smithfield, EC1 to be picked up by poor widows of the parish. Tradition says a benefactress, whose name is forgotten, left a sum of money in her will for that purpose but the gift was lost and the senior church warden had to supply the coins from his own pocket. The charity was put on a firm footing through the generosity of Joshua Whitehead Butterworth in the 19th century who made the gift a "matter of continuity for all future time" and dedicated to the pious memory of a late Rector of the church, the Rev. William Panckridge. Every Good Friday at 1130 hrs, a presentation of hot cross buns and coins is made to poor widows, nowadays to local children, the gifts being laid on tomb stones outside the West door of the church. (See also Easter Parade)

Public welcome to attend.

CART MARKING

This ceremony has recently been revived and is now the scene of some spectacular vintage and modern vehicles assembled in Guildhall Yard, EC2 for a re-enactment of the original ceremony. The ceremony takes place in July or August and originally involved the branding by a hot iron of a registration number and the City's coat of arms on a vehicle. It dates from 1681 when the number of carts plying their trade in the City was limited to 421. At one time the fee for this service went to Christ's Hospital but in 1838 the duty was transferred to the Keeper of Guildhall and the branding now takes the form of a metal plate.

The public are welcome to watch the ceremony which takes place at approximately 1200 hrs – arrive early to watch the carts assemble in Guildhall Yard.

CEREMONY OF THE KEYS

The 700-year old ceremonial locking of the main gate of the Tower of London is carried out each evening by the Chief Yeoman Warder of the Tower, accompanied by an escort of Guard.

At seven minutes before 2200 hrs, the Chief Warder, in his long red coat and Tudor bonnet, carrying in one hand a candle lantern and in the other the Queen's Keys, leaves the Byward Tower and proceeds to Traitors' Gate where an escort, normally provided by one of the regiment of Foot Guards, awaits him. He hands the lantern to a member of the escort and the party moves to the outer gate, the first to be locked. Along the route all guards and sentries salute the Queen's Keys. Still with his escort, the Chief Warder returns towards Water Lane. The great oak doors of the Middle and Byward Towers are locked and the Procession retraces its steps to the archway of the Bloody Tower, where a sentry issues the challenge, 'Halt! Who goes there?' The Chief Warder answers, 'The Keys'. 'Whose Keys?', comes the query. 'Queen Elizabeth's Keys'. 'Pass Queen Elizabeth's Keys. All's well'. The party passes on under the archway to where the main guard is drawn up. The officer in charge gives the command to present arms. The Chief Warder moves two paces forward, lifts his Tudor bonnet and cries,

'God preserve Queen Elizabeth'. The clock is chiming 2200 hrs as the guard answers 'Amen' and the bugler sounds the Last Post. Finally the Warder delivers the keys to the Queen's House and the guard is dismissed.

Applications for tickets should be addressed to: The Resident Governor and Keeper of the Jewel House, Queen's House, HM Tower of London, EC3N 4AB. Please quote name, date required, number of people (max. 7), as many alternative dates as possible and enclose a stamped, addressed envelope. (Tickets are free of charge.)

YEOMAN WARDER

With his Tudor bonnet of black velvet trimmed with the ribbons of the Queen's colours, the Yeoman Warder at the Tower probably makes the most outstanding of all London's traditional characters. Around his neck he wears a ruff of bleached Irish linen buttoned at the back with its hem tucked into the collar of his scarlet coat. The coat is embellished at the skirt, sleeves and sword belt with lines of gold braid on strips of black velvet. On the chest and back are the royal symbols of the crown and heraldic Tudor rose with the thistle and shamrock and the letters "ER" (Elizabeth Regina) embroidered in gold thread. The scarlet britches are held tight below the knee by gold braid and the dress is complete with scarlet stockings and black shoes.

CHANGING THE GUARD

The protection of the Sovereign has been the responsibility of the Household Division, made up of the Household Cavalry and the five regiments of Foot Guards, since the Restoration of the Monarchy after the Civil War in 1660.

Today guard mounting takes place in London at four royal palaces, and at Windsor Castle just outside London.

The Tower of London was the first royal London residence until Henry VIII settled at Whitehall Palace in the 17th Century. This burned down in 1698 leaving just Banqueting House. The Queen's Life Guard still mount daily at Horseguards Arch opposite, regarded as the official entrance to the royal palaces. After the fire the Sovereign moved to St. James's Palace across the park. This remains the centre of the Court and even today foreign ambassadors are "accredited to the Court of St. James". Queen Victoria chose Buckingham Palace, or Buckingham House as it was then known, as her new royal residence when she came to the throne in 1837 and it has remained the main London residence of the Sovereign ever since. It is here that the most impressive Guard Changing ceremony takes place.

CHANGING THE GUARD AT BUCKINGHAM PALACE

At 1100 hrs the St. James's Palace detachment of the Old Guard is inspected in Friary Court and then marches off via the Mall carrying the Colour (the regimental flag). At Buckingham Palace the Buckingham Palace detachment is lined up and inspected. The St. James's detachment enters by the South Gate and together they await the arrival of the New Guard. At 1130 hrs the New Guard, led by a regimental band, marches into the Palace forecourt via the North Centre Gate having earlier formed up at nearby Wellington Barracks in Birdcage Walk.

The New Guard advances towards the Old Guard to the appropriate music and in a symbolic ceremony the Palace keys are handed to the New Guard. While the sentries are being changed music is played – in all for some 30 minutes. At 1205 hrs the Guards are reformed and the Old Guard leaves by the centre gates and marches off to the barracks. The St. James's detachment of the New Guard marches off at 1207 hrs with the Colour which is lodged in the Officers' Guardroom off Ambassadors Court.

Good places to watch are outside St. James's Palace, walking behind the Old Guard to Buckingham Palace, or in Birdcage Walk watching the New Guard forming up. Outside the Gates of Buckingham Palace it can be crowded.

Parties of British school-children are allowed inside the railings of Buckingham Palace for Changing the Guard on application to: Master of the Household, Buckingham Palace, SW1.

This ceremony takes place every day from April to the end of July and every other day from August to the end of March approximately and is cancelled in wet weather.

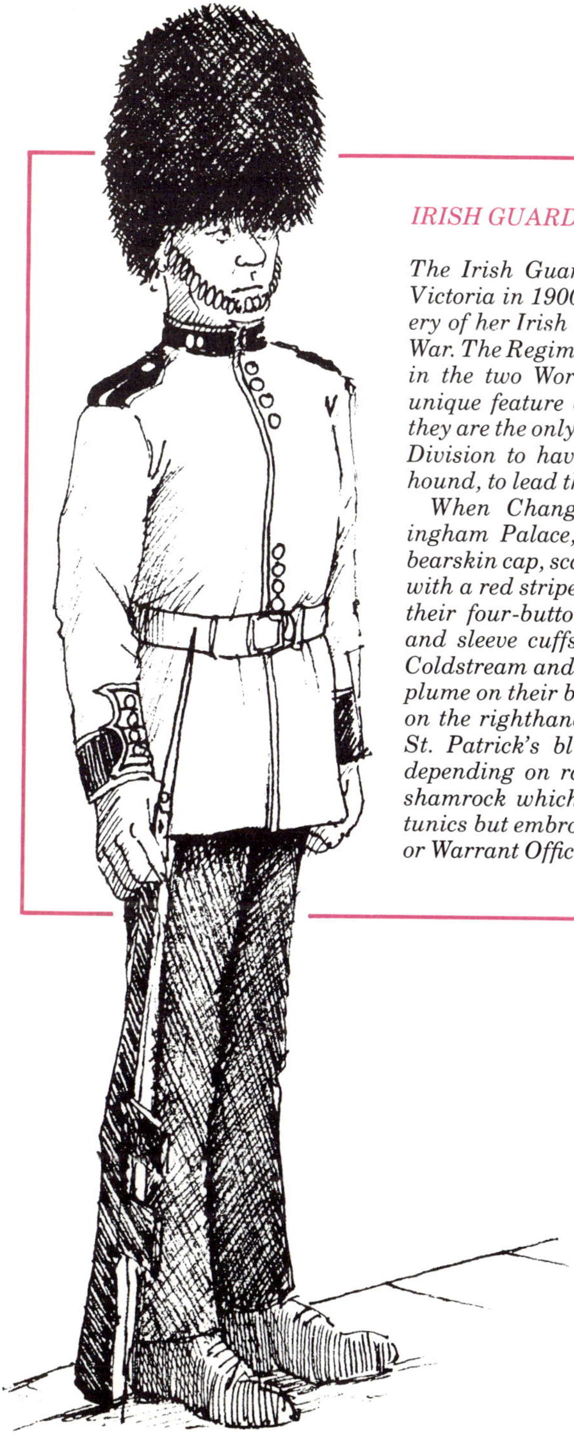

IRISH GUARDS

The Irish Guards were formed by Queen Victoria in 1900 in recognition of the bravery of her Irish troops in the South African War. The Regiment won six Victoria Crosses in the two World Wars of this century. A unique feature of the Irish Guards is that they are the only Regiment in the Household Division to have a Mascot, an Irish Wolfhound, to lead them on parade.

When Changing the Guard at Buckingham Palace, the Irish Guards wear a bearskin cap, scarlet tunic and blue trousers with a red stripe. They can be recognised by their four-button groupings on the tunics and sleeve cuffs and, like the Grenadiers, Coldstream and Welsh Guards, they wear a plume on their bearskin caps. This plume is on the righthand side and consists of 6" of St. Patrick's blue cut feathers or bristle, depending on rank. The collar badge is a shamrock which is white on Guardsmen's tunics but embroidered in silver on Officers' or Warrant Officers' tunics.

CHANGING THE GUARD AT WHITEHALL, TOWER OF LONDON AND WINDSOR CASTLE

The mounted New Guard leaves Hyde Park Barracks at 1028 hrs on weekdays and 0928 hrs on Sundays, riding down the Mall to Whitehall. The Guard is provided alternately by the Life Guards and the Blues and Royals. The New Guard arrives at 1100 hrs on weekdays, 1000 hrs on Sundays, forming up facing the Old Guard in Horseguards (summer months) and Tilt Yard in the winter, saluting their respective Standards. The two sentries in the boxes facing Whitehall are posted. The Old Guard forms up and moves off down the Mall to the barracks. There is no music. This ceremony is held daily.

The regiment which provides the Queen's Guard for the day also provides the Guard for the Tower of London. The ceremony at the Tower only takes place when the Court is in residence at Buckingham Palace. The Guard is mounted on Tower Green at noon. (See also Ceremony of the Keys).

The Guardmounting Ceremony at Windsor Castle takes place at 1100 hrs in the Quadrangle if the court is in residence or, when Her Majesty is not in residence, on Castle Hill in the summer months and outside the guardroom in winter. The ceremony in the Quadrangle is accompanied by music. Guardmounting takes place every day in summer and alternates with the guard change at Buckingham Palace in the winter.

CHARLES I COMMEMORATION

On 30 January 1649 King Charles I was led to his death at the scaffold through a window of Banqueting House in Whitehall. This event is commemorated each year on the last Sunday in January by the King's Army (the Royalist Wing of the English Civil War Society) dressed and armed in totally authentic mid-17th century style.

The procession assembles outside St. James's Palace at 1100 hrs. Leaving at 1130 hrs, it makes its way down The Mall, through Horse Guards, to the Banqueting House in Whitehall, following the route of Charles' last walk. Here a short service of commemoration is held and a wreath is laid at 1200 hrs beneath the window through which Charles stepped onto the scaffold. This is followed by the presentation of the King's Army service awards and the Commissioning of Officers. The parade then marches to Trafalgar Square, past the statue of Charles I, where a wreath has previously been laid, through Admiralty Arch and back down The Mall to St. James's Palace arriving at approximately 1245 hrs, where the parade is dismissed.

Banqueting House: Open 1000-1700 hrs Tuesday to Saturday, 1400-1700 hrs Sunday. Admission 70p adults, 35p under 16s and OAPs.

Leaflet available from the English Civil War Society, 70 Hailgate, Howden, North Humberside DN14 7ST.

LIFE GUARDS

The Life Guards are the senior, though not the oldest, regiment of the British Army. At the end of the Civil War, a number of Royalists followed Prince Charles (later Charles II) into exile, and in Holland, 80 of them were organised into a body of Life Guards, of whom 20 were always on duty to guard the Royal residence or escort Charles. The Life Guards have a distinguished fighting record and have participated in many of the major battles and campaigns of the British Army. To this day, the duties of mounting the Sovereign's Life Guard and providing the Sovereign's Escort have remained their two principal functions. When they are taking part in the Changing the Guard ceremony at Horse Guards, or providing the Sovereign's Escort on ceremonial occasions, the Life Guards wear full dress uniform, the pattern and style of which has changed little since 1856. They wear scarlet tunics and white helmet plumes and white, close-fitting leather breeches. The white cross belts are worn over the left shoulder and have a flash-cord running down the centre. The steel cuirass of breast and back plates, worn by both the Life Guards and the Blues and Royals, is the only body armour still worn by any British soldier. The boots are highly-polished thigh boots and the cloak worn in winter or bad weather covers not only the rider but also the haunches of the horse.

BLUES AND ROYALS

The sister regiment of the Life Guards in the Household Cavalry was the Royal Horse Guards (The Blues). However, in 1969, The Blues were amalgamated with another of the British Army, the Royal Dragoons (the First Dragoons). They formed a new regiment in the Household Cavalry, known as the Blues and Royals. When they are Changing the Guard at Buckingham Palace and attending state occasions, they wear full dress uniform – blue tunics, red helmet plumes and white leather breeches. White cross belts are worn over the left shoulder and the cuirasses and leather boots are identical to those of the Life Guards.

CHELSEA FLOWER SHOW

The Chelsea Flower Show has been held since 1913, in late May, in the grounds of the Royal Hospital, Chelsea. The Royal Horticultural Society promotes the show to educate and instruct gardeners and the public and to provide an international exhibition covering every aspect of gardening. There are over 360 exhibitors, including many from overseas, making the Chelsea Flower Show the largest of its kind in the world. A huge marquee is erected to cover three and a half acres, in which plants and flowers of all seasons are shown; they are forced or retarded to be at their best for the four days of the Show. Garden furniture, tools, theme gardens, greenhouses and gardening books are also on display and there is an advice bureau for help in solving gardening problems. Many of the plants and flowers on show are sold to the public on the last day.

Entrance on the first day is restricted to members of the Royal Horticultural Society, but anyone can join the Society at the gate on that day. To avoid crowds, come at 0800 hrs or after 1600 hrs. Admission prices decrease after 1600 hrs on Wednesday and Thursday. Children under the age of five and dogs are not admitted. Details from the Royal Horticultural Society on 01-834 4333.

CHINESE NEW YEAR FESTIVITIES

London's Chinese community has based itself in the Soho area, evidence of which is clearly visible from the many Chinese restaurants and food shops. New Year is the highlight of the Chinese year. It is not on a set date, but is based on cycles of the moon and falls in late January or early February. On the Sunday nearest the date of the New Year, the area of Soho around Newport Place and Gerrard and Lisle Streets comes alive from midday until the early hours of Monday morning with decorations, streamers and garlands adorning and hanging from windows and balconies in the streets. Large crowds are attracted by the famous Lion Dances, when young men don the colourful costume and weave their way through the streets while the "Lion" receives gifts of money and food from residents and restaurants en route.

1987 is the Year of the Rabbit. In 1988, the date for the Chinese New Year is 17 February and it will be the Year of the Dragon.

CHRIST'S HOSPITAL SERVICE

In late September each year the boys from Christ's Hospital School, Horsham (the "Bluecoat Boys"), dressed in their traditional uniform of blue cassocks and yellow socks, and led by the school band walk from London Bridge Station to the Church of St. Sepulchre High Holborn, WC1 for the St. Matthew's Day service at 1100 hrs. Christ's Hospital dates from 1552 when Bishop Ridley preached an impassioned sermon before King Edward VI at Westminster Abbey on the needs of the poor. As a result, the King ordered three institutions for the poor to be built of which Christ's Hospital was destined for orphans and children of the poor. The service originates from a requirement that a list of governors has to be handed to the Lord

Mayor of London once a year. Included in the service is a reading by a distinguished Old Blue. Afterwards, at approximately 1200 hrs, the boys make their way through the City streets to Mansion House where they each receive a gift of freshly minted coins from the Lord Mayor.

Very limited space is available to the general public for the service itself. However, it is easy for visitors to watch the walk to Mansion House anywhere along the route.

CHRISTMAS TREE AND LIGHTS

Since 1947 the City of Oslo has presented a Norwegian spruce Christmas tree as an expression of goodwill towards London and of gratitude for help given by Britain during World War II.

The tree is erected in Trafalgar Square, normally from mid-December and is decorated in white lights – Norwegian style – lit from approximately 1500 hrs to 2400 hrs until Twelfth Night. Carols are sung around the tree each evening until Christmas Eve by groups in aid of many charities.

Christmas lights are switched on in Regent Street and Oxford Street from mid-November, normally until Twelfth Night.

Please check with LTB on 01-730 3488 nearer the time for dates.

Fires and lights, symbols of warmth and everlasting life, have always been associated with Christmas, both pagan and Christian. Evergreens, as symbols of survival, have a long association with Christmas festivities, probably dating from the 8th century when St. Boniface completed the Christianisation of Germany and dedicated the fir tree to the Holy Child to replace the sacred oak of Odin. The Christmas tree was made popular after Queen Victoria and Prince Albert (a great enthusiast for the customs of his country) included a tree, decorated with candles, tinsel and ornaments in the German manner, amongst their Christmas celebrations in 1841.

Each year (usually in December) HM the Queen gives two trees to St. Paul's which stand inside the Cathedral.

For dates, contact the Cathedral nearer the time on 01-236 4128.

CLOG AND APRON RACE

The Clog and Apron Race is held at Kew Gardens, Richmond, Surrey at the end of September each year (normally the last Thursday). Starting at approximately 1730 hrs, the race is run along the full length of the Broad Walk – a wide 375-yard avenue running between the Palm House Pond and the Orangery.

The race originates from the custom that all the first year horticultural students and gardeners working under glass were issued with a pair of wooden-soled leather clogs and a navy blue gardening apron which, with a budding knife tucked into the large apron pocket, were worn with pride as symbols of office. Clogs were better than leather boots for keeping feet dry on the wet greenhouse floor and, even today, some clogs are still issued.

The race is thought to have started in the 1920s, although adequate records have only been kept since the 1940s. All those taking part today are horticultural students working at the Gardens; women are given a 50-yard

continued overleaf

start on the race. Despite the weight of the clogs fastest time is just 60 seconds!

Nearest gates for entry are the Main Gate and Victoria Gate. For dates contact Kew Gardens nearer the time on 01-940 1171.

CLOWN'S SERVICE

This colourful and surprising event is held on the first Sunday in February, usually at Holy Trinity Church, Dalston, E8. It attracts many members of Clowns International Club, whose church this is and who attend in full costume and traditional make-up. During the service, which begins at 1600 hrs, a wreath is laid on the memorial to Grimaldi who originated the clown character and outfit as we now know them. A free clown show is given afterwards in the church hall and all visitors are welcome.

Grimaldi was buried in 1837 at St. James's Church, Pentonville Road, N1. Although the church is no longer standing, the churchyard can still be visited. It is now known as Grimaldi Park and there is a plaque marking the famous clown's tomb.

Check with LTB on 01-730 3488 for exact date.

COURT OF COMMON COUNCIL

This is the City's "parliament" and it is arguable whether or not it pre-dates the House of Commons. The Court of Common Council began in the 12th century as an informal consultation with the Mayor and Aldermen on "common affairs" with its members representing each one of the 26 wards in the City. By 1384 it became elective and gained its real power in the 17th century. There are now some 130 members of the Court of Common Council still representing the same number of wards. Their function is the same as that of any other local authority operating within a committee structure whose major decisions are put before the Court's meetings held every third Thursday, at approximately 1300 hrs in Guildhall, EC2.

The meetings are usually quite short and the general public are admitted free of charge. Visitors arriving before 1245 hrs can benefit from a short talk explaining the work of the Council and the role they play in City affairs. For dates, telephone 01-606 3030.

COURT OF HUSTING

This is one of the oldest ceremonies in the City and dates from the 10th century. Nowadays it is convened only at irregular intervals but once the Court of Hustings had wide powers in civil and criminal cases. Nowadays its purpose is the enrolment of the Corporation's Trust Deeds. It is a reflection on the position of women in mediaeval society that men who did not surrender to the Court when summoned five times were outlawed whereas women, having no status within the law anywhere, were "waived" – dispossessed and turned into waifs.

MORRIS DANCING

London has many Morris "sides" or teams who attend various gatherings – fairs, festivals and charity events throughout the year. Each team has a series of dances that have been drawn on and added to the traditional dance to which the earliest reference is from the 15th century. The dances are often performed wielding heavy sticks, slings or handkerchiefs and are accompanied by pipe, tabor, melodian, concertina or fiddle. Often the dances are accompanied by extra non-dancing characters such as animals or fools.

The colourful and varied costumes can be made up using any combination of the following items – clogs, straw hats, jackets made of rags, blacked-out faces, rosettes, white shirts, bells, top hats and shoes with buckles. Women may wear alternate coloured leggings, bells on ankles and wrists, embroidered smocks, blue faces, white shirts and rosettes.

Regular displays of Morris Dancing take place from Mid-May to Mid-August each year on Broad Sanctuary in front of Westminster Abbey from 1915 hrs every Wednesday. Details of where and when to watch dancing can be obtained by writing to the Bagman at The London Morris Club, c/o Cecil Sharp House, 2 Regent's Park Road, NW1.

CROMWELL'S DAY

A service is held on 3 September each year, starting at 1500 hrs at the statue of Oliver Cromwell on Cromwell Green outside the Houses of Parliament. This is arranged by the Cromwell Association to pay tribute to the famous Puritan Statesman on the anniversary of his death (1659); hymns are sung and an address is given by a distinguished Cromwellian.

Further details from the Cromwell Association on 01-435 2391.

DERBY

A festival of racing featuring the Derby, one of the greatest horse races in the world for three year old colts and fillies, takes place on the Wednesday of the first week in June.

Derby Day, which has been run since 1780, has a tremendous atmosphere, with crowds of London families taking an excursion for the day, and trying their luck with the "bookies". A funfair sets up on Epsom Downs for the week, providing entertainment well into the evening.

Tickets are available from 1 January from: The Secretary, Racecourse Paddock, Epsom, Surrey. Tel: Epsom (03727) 26311.

DICKENS'S READING AND CAROL SERVICE

This no longer takes place regularly, contact LTB for information.

DOGGETT'S COAT AND BADGE RACE

The Doggett's Coat & Badge Race was founded in 1714 by Thomas Doggett, a popular Irish comedian. This famous sculling race normally takes place on a day in July and is a four and a half mile course from London Bridge to Chelsea. The winner wears a distinctive scarlet uniform and silver badge.

This race for single sculls, owes its origin to Thomas Doggett's difficulty one stormy night, in finding a boat to take him home after the theatre – a Thames journey up-river against the tide. It was a young Waterman who had just completed his apprenticeship, who eventually rowed him to Chelsea. The incident later inspired Doggett to found a race rowed against the tide for first year Freemen of London.

Contact Mr. Earl, Fishmongers' Company on 01-626 3531.

DRUID EQUINOXES

The Druid Order still celebrates Equinox ceremonies in Spring and Autumn. The Spring Equinox ceremony following ancient ritual, is held in March on Tower Hill Terrace at 1200 hrs and celebrates the season of planting and renewal. Seeds are sown and are symbolic of ideas and feelings. The Autumn Equinox is held in September at 1300 hrs on Primrose Hill, Regent's Park, NW3 and celebrates the coming of the Harvest season. The Lady of Autumn scatters fruit on the ground, which goes back into the earth carrying the seeds for the next Spring Equinox.

Contact LTB on 01-730 3488 nearer the time for dates.

DOGGETTS COAT AND BADGE

The Doggetts Coat and Badge is awarded to the winner of the Doggetts Coat and Badge Race and consists of a scarlet knee-length, skirted-tunic uniform with a large silver badge on the left arm. Since the early days of the race, changes have taken place – the coat is nearer to red than orange and the handmade badge is inscribed with the name of the winner, the date and year of his win. Fine examples of this uniform can be seen at the National Maritime Museum at Greenwich.

DUNKIRK VETERANS SERVICE

An annual service is held each year at 1500 hrs on a Sunday in May at the Church of St. Lawrence Jewry-next-Guildhall, Gresham Street, EC2, to which spectators are welcome.

At 1430 hrs, Veterans of the Dunkirk evacuation of World War II march from Swan Court to the church. There is a procession of standards and a casket containing sand from the beach at Dunkirk is placed on the altar. After the service, wreaths are laid and the parade is inspected. They then march to Armoury House in City Road, arriving at 1630 hrs.

Public welcome to attend.

BARGEMASTER

The ceremonial uniform of the bargemaster includes a fore and aft peaked black hat with the coat of arms of the Fishmongers' Company. He wears a maroon tunic with blue facings and gold badges. The most distinctive part of the uniform is the large brass coloured badge worn on the sleeve with the coat of arms of the Fishmongers' Company. The uniform is completed by navy blue trousers and shoes.

EASTER PARADE

The first Easter Parade in Battersea Park took place in 1962; a forerunner had been held in 1959 in Hyde Park. The event had no real historic background other than the organiser's wish to create a new, jolly event for Londoners. It was started by the London Tourist Board and took place every year, later organised by the Greater London Council and from 1987 by the London Borough of Wandsworth. The coming of Spring had traditionally been marked by people "walking about" showing off their new clothes on Easter Sunday and the Easter Parade in New York's Central Park has become famous. London's parade also has its Easter bonnets and Easter Princess competition with celebrities as judges. Regimental bands, London personalities, animals, flower floats and jazz bands are part of the Parade which takes place every Easter Sunday around the Park's perimeter, usually starting at 1500 hrs, with entertainment and sideshows throughout the Park from mid-day.

For other Easter customs see Pancake Day, Maundy Money, Hot Cross Bun Ceremony, Spital Sermon and Butterworth Charity.

EPIPHANY GIFTS

On Twelfth Day, 6 January, the journey of the Magi, the Three Wise Men of the East, is remembered in all Christian churches, but nowhere is the Feast of Epiphany celebrated with greater tradition than in the Chapel Royal of St. James's Palace, SW1 where, for over 900 years, the service has been re-enacting the offerings of the Magi. Two Gentlemen Ushers to the Queen now represent the Sovereign at the Chapel Royal and the Bishop of London receives and dedicates the offerings.

At 1130 hrs, the service opens with a procession of the choir and clergy followed by a detachment of the Yeomen of the Guard; the National Anthem is sung. The Holy Communion Service then commences and after the Creed an appropriate Anthem (often "The Three Kings" by Cornelius) indicates that the moment has come for the presentation of the offerings. From the west door, the Serjeant of the Vestry, bearing his silver-gilt wand, leads the two Gentlemen Ushers to the altar. They carry the traditional gifts of gold, frankincense and myrrh. Behind them comes the escort (the Serjeant Major and two Yeomen of the Guard) and the procession stops three times for the Gentlemen Ushers to bow to the altar. These offerings are then dedicated and laid on the altar. The Queen's representatives retire, again turning and bowing, and the offertory hymn follows. At the close of the hymn the Yeomen of the Guard retire and the Communion Service continues.

Admission for the service is by ticket only, available in writing from: Serjeant of the Vestry, St. James's Palace, London SW1.

CHELSEA PENSIONERS

The Royal Hospital, Chelsea, has approximately 420 In-Pensioners, divided into six companies. Men over 65 (55 if unable to earn a living) are boarded, lodged, clothed, nursed when ill and retain their state pensions. Their uniform consists of two scarlet coats which in design date from the 18th century. A tricorne hat is worn on special occasions, such as Oak Apple Day (Founder's Day). The In-Pensioners still wear their old Regimental badges on their caps within the precincts of the Royal Hospital. When walking outside the precincts, they wear a cap bearing the letters R.H.

FARTHING BUNDLES

This custom of distributing toys to children in the East End of London, was founded by Miss Clara Grant at her Fern Street Settlement in Bromley by Bow in 1907 to provide playthings for the children of the area. While they were not offered "charity", each child who passed under the four-foot high wooden arch could buy a "bundle" wrapped in newspaper for a farthing (¼ of a penny), later 1 penny. The arch is still in use but now increased in height to take account of today's taller children and bears the words "Enter all ye children small; None can come who are too tall". The original settlement has now been demolished and increasing affluence has reduced the need for such gestures.

The ceremony carries on at the new settlement at Leadenham Court, Spanby Road, E3 on special occasions. It will take place in September 1987 to celebrate its 80th anniversary. Telephone 01-987 1949 nearer the time for the date.

FIREWORKS NIGHT

Guy Fawkes was arrested by Yeomen of the Guard on 5 November 1605, just one of the conspirators in the "Gunpowder Plot" to blow up King James I and his Parliament. To this day, the Yeomen of the Guard, the oldest Royal Bodyguard and the oldest military Corps in the world, make an annual search of the cellars of the Houses of Parliament prior to the State Opening of Parliament.

For this duty, the Guard, equipped with lanterns, carry out a ceremonial tour of the cellars – traditionally ensuring that no 20th century Guy Fawkes is lurking beneath the Palace of Westminster with kegs of gunpowder.

The anniversary of Guy Fawkes' death is widely commemorated with a number of organised firework displays with bonfires on which effigies of Guy Fawkes are burnt.

For details of displays in the London area, contact LTB on 01-730 3488 nearer the time.

FOUNDER'S DAY

The Royal Hospital, Chelsea, SW3 was founded in 1682 by King Charles II to house old soldiers who must be of good character and in receipt of an Army Pension for either long service or disability. Army pensioners admitted to the Royal Hospital are called "In-Pensioners" and all other Army pensioners are "Out-Pensioners".

The In-Pensioners parade once a year on Founder's Day at approximately 1100 hrs. This used to be on 29 May, Oak Apple Day (Charles II's birthday and the anniversary of his restoration to the throne). Nowadays, the parade takes place on the first Thursday after 29 May. The In-Pensioners parade in their traditional uniforms of scarlet coat and black tricorne hat. The King's statue is decorated with oak leaves and all In-Pensioners and spectators wear a sprig of oak leaves – symbols of the oak tree in which Charles II hid whilst escaping after the Battle of Worcester during the English Civil War.

This is a private ceremony and admission is by invitation only.

GARTER SERVICE

The Queen is Sovereign of all orders of Chivalry, of which the oldest and most prestigious is the Most Noble Order of the Garter, founded by Edward III in 1348. The Order of the Garter is reserved for members of the Royal Family, foreign royalty and statesmen.

Almost every year, the Knights attend a service at St. George's Chapel, Windsor, on a day in mid-June, when any new knights are invested. The Chapel closes to the public for a few days before the ceremony for preparations, and on the day of the ceremony itself the grounds of Windsor Castle are also closed to the general public.

The Queen usually decides the date in January and this is then published.

Although the ceremony is private, it is possible to apply for tickets between 1 January and 28 February to stand within the precincts to, The Lord Chamberlain's Office, St. James's Palace, London SW1.

SHERIFFS' FOOTMEN

Each of the two Sheriff's has a footman who are normally based at the Central Criminal Court where one of the Sheriff's has to be in daily attendance. The footmen wear a maroon-coloured short tail jacket, heavily trimmed with gold thread. On the jacket sleeve is an embroidered Corporation's coat of arms. The waistcoat is maroon and around the neck they wear a white stock. Knee breeches, white stockings and buckled court shoes complete their splendid outfit.

GUN SALUTES

Gun salutes are fired in Hyde Park, W1 (opposite the Dorchester Hotel), by the King's Troop, Royal Horse Artillery and at the Tower of London by the Honourable Artillery Company. No salute is ever fired on a Sunday, therefore if any of the dates fall on the Sunday, the salute is held over to the next day.

In Hyde Park, six guns and limbers are driven to the Park and for the salute up to 70 horses and men take part in the operation. The soldiers gallop their horses down to the saluting station, pulling their massive gun carriages behind them, set them up, then fire. The number of rounds fired for a Royal salute varies according to location. The King's Troop fire a 41 gun salute in Hyde Park (no other unit has the privilege of firing a gun salute in Hyde Park) – 21 guns as a Royal Salute and 20 for the capital. (When a Royal Salute is fired in the Home Park at Windsor, this is a normal 21 gun Royal Salute.) The Honourable Artillery Company fire a Royal Salute of 62 rounds at the Tower of London (no other unit has the privilege of firing a gun salute at the Tower of London) – 41 rounds in view of the fact that the Tower is still regarded as a royal residence and another 21 rounds for the City of London. Gun salutes are fired at 1200 hrs in Hyde Park and at 1300 hrs at the Tower of London on the following dates:

6 February – Accession Day; 21 April – Queen's Birthday; 2 June – Coronation Day; 10 June – Prince Philip's Birthday; 4 August – Queen Mother's Birthday.

Gun salutes also take place for Trooping the Colour, State Opening of Parliament and some State Visits. Times for these salutes vary so please check in advance with LTB on 01-730 3488.

HARNESS HORSE PARADE

Regent's Park is the venue for a rather different sort of parade on Easter Monday. The London Harness Horse Parade provides an opportunity to see just how many working horses there still are, even in these days of mechanisation – and to see them at their best, competing for prizes of rosettes, brass merit badges and prize cards.

The programme begins at approximately 0930 hrs, with veterinary inspections followed by the main parade. Next comes the judging of such classes as Heavy Horses, Single Horsed Commercial Vans and Private Turnouts. Events end with a Grand Parade of winners at 1200 hrs until about 1300 hrs.

This event amalgamated in 1966 from two parades – the London Cart Horse and the London Van Horse Parades. It is not a competition between entries, but for each entry to reach a certain standard of turnout. Owners of private driving vehicles can also now join the parade, so many different types of vehicles and animals are to be seen at this free event.

For information telephone: 01-870 0141.

HARVEST OF THE SEA

This thanksgiving service has been held in the Church of St. Mary-at-Hill, Lovat Lane, Eastcheap, EC3, on the second Sunday in October since the 17th century. St. Mary-at-Hill is the church of the former Billingsgate fish market in Lower Thames Street. A great slab placed in the porch was decorated with almost every available species of fish sold in the market by the Billingsgate traders. The church was decorated with nets and items connected with the sea. The fish on display was later donated to charity.

Today the fish merchants from the new Billingsgate Market on the Isle of Dogs continue the tradition by delivering a tremendous variety of fish, which is displayed in the vestibule. The service at 1100 hrs is usually attended by the Aldermen and Common Councilmen of the Ward, who come in State. After the service, the fish will go to Church Army hostels for the aged throughout London. The reason for this is that Prebendary Carlile, founder of the Church Army, was once Rector of St. Mary-at-Hill.

Public welcome to attend.

HEAD OF THE RIVER RACE

The Head of the River Race is a processional race for eights, rowed over the University Boat Race course from Mortlake to Putney on the third or fourth Saturday in March each year, the starting time varying according to tides. For safety reasons, the entry is limited to 420 crews who start one behind the other at 10-second intervals, the winner being the crew which returns the fastest time. The record time is 16 minutes 37 seconds, set up by the Amateur Rowing Association National Squad First Crew in 1987.

The first race was run in 1920 with 23 crews and was the idea of the Cambridge and Tideway Oarsman Steve Fairburn and was originally intended to give tideway crews a goal to work towards in order to make

continued overleaf

winter training worthwhile. The race attracts entries from rowing clubs all over Great Britain and many from Europe, particularly West Germany. It lasts about 1½ hours and one of the best ways to see it is to stand on the Surrey bank above Chiswick Bridge about half-an-hour before the start and then to walk along the towpath towards Putney.

For dates phone 01-940 1171 x 4112.

HENLEY ROYAL REGATTA

Henley-on-Thames, Oxfordshire, is the setting for the famous Henley International Rowing Regatta, held annually since 1839, during the week culminating on the 27th Sunday of the year (in July).

The Regatta is rowed on a course upstream, against the current, running for one mile, 550 yards from Temple Island to just below Henley Bridge.

Tickets, subject to availability, can be obtained from The Secretary, Regatta Headquarters, Henley-on-Thames, Oxfordshire RG9 2LY. Tel: Henley-on-Thames (0491) 572153.

HENRY WOOD PROMENADE CONCERTS

Founded in 1895, the 'Proms' were the brainchild of a London impressario, Robert Newman, whose ambition, along with a young conductor, Henry Wood, was to help people discover and enjoy 'serious' music. The idea of Proms – concerts with an informal atmosphere where the 'promenade' audience could walk around and come and go freely, was a concept that originated in France in the 1830s. Newman's plan for Prom Seasons was to offer Londoners an enormous variety of music nightly for two months at a price they could afford. Originally held in the Queen's Hall in London, the Proms were transferred in 1941 to the Royal Albert Hall following a bombing raid which destroyed their former home.

Henry Wood planned and conducted his first Prom season in 1895 and continued his involvement with the Proms until 1944, when he invited the BBC to present the concerts after his retirement.

Today, Proms seasons are usually held for eight weeks, July to September and welcome international soloists and orchestras from all over the world, though the BBC Symphony Orchestra, along with the BBC Philharmonic, BBC Welsh and BBC Scottish Symphony Orchestras still undertake the major share of the concerts.

Both season and individual seat tickets are available in advance from Prom Concerts Box Office, Royal Albert Hall, SW7 2AR.

Last Night – subject to availability, up to two seats per applicant are allocated to those who apply at the same time for at least four other concerts in the season.

HISTORIC COMMERCIAL VEHICLE RUN

Since 1962, on the first Sunday in May, a group of historic vehicles has set out from Battersea Park, SW11 from 0630 hrs to drive along the A23 to Madeira Drive, Brighton. Unlike the RAC Veteran Car Run, these are all commercial vehicles – buses, fire engines, delivery vans and military vehicles and they provide quite a spectacle as their drivers battle to reach the finish. The vehicles are on display in Battersea Park as part of The Wheels of Yesterday Rally, starting on the Saturday. This is three days of vehicle parades, model steam railways, steam funfair, Punch & Judy shows and many more activities.

Visitors are welcome – no charge.

HORSEMAN'S SUNDAY

A service for "The Blessing of the Horses" is quite traditional in Britain, giving an opportunity for horse-people to get together in a quiet, respectful manner.

Horseman's Sunday in London is held on the second last Sunday in September every year and was started in 1968 by Ross Nye, when local riding stables were being threatened with closure. Horses assemble from 1130 hrs at the Church of St. John and St. Michael, Hyde Park Crescent, W2 until the commencement of the service at 1200 hrs. The service, which is taken by the vicar on horseback, lasts approximately 25 minutes followed by a procession of the horses, singly and in pairs, to receive commemorative rosettes, ending at 1300 hrs. Following the presentation of rosettes, the horses continue on into Hyde Park for an outing on the 2½ miles of riding tracks.

In addition, there is a Horse Show in Kensington Paddock (the western end of Kensington Gardens) from 1330 hrs onwards which includes showing classes, showjumping and gymkhana events.

Contact Ross Nye on 01-262 3791.

HOT CROSS BUN CEREMONY

A rather sad tradition is carried out at the Widow's Son Inn, 75 Devons Road, Bow, E3 every Good Friday at 1300 hrs. Some 200 years ago a cottage stood on the site of this tavern, occupied by a widow whose only son was a sailor. Expecting him home one Easter, she laid aside a hot cross bun on Good Friday. He did not return and no news of his death was received. The widow, refusing to despair, kept the buns and added a new one each Good Friday to the cluster hanging from a beam in her cottage. When the pub replaced the cottage, the custom was continued and every Good Friday a sailor or Wren adds a new bun to the blackened collection.

Public welcome to watch.

INDIAN FESTIVALS

The Sanskritik Festival of the Arts of India is normally held in July at the South Bank Concert Halls. This is a series of individual programmes of songs, music, dance and drums, performed in classical and traditional styles from the many regions of India. The Festival provides audiences with the rare opportunity to experience and enjoy India's rich cultural heritage through its dancers, music and songs.

For dates contact the South Bank nearer the time on 01-928 3191.

Diwali, Festival of Lights, is a religious festival celebrating the death of the demon Narak at the hand of the deity Lord Krishna. Normally taking place in November, this festival is four days of festivities which include dancing, singing and exhibitions. A special service is held in temples throughout London on the last day at 1900 hrs, beginning with the worship of the deity Lord Krishna, after which devotional songs are sung and candles are lit (hence the name Festival of Lights). Sweets are distributed amongst the congregation after the service. Diwali is celebrated in Indian communities throughout London. The public are welcome to attend the service which is held at the Institute of Indian Culture, 4a Castletown Road, West Kensington, W14.

Further details are available from the Institute on 01-381 3086.

JEWISH FESTIVALS

Many events and activities take place in local Jewish communities, of which two are listed below.

Israel Independence Day is celebrated in April or May each year with activities such as torchlight processions, fairs, traditional Israeli dancing and musical events.

Purim, the Feast of Lots, is celebrated in March each year when many fancy dress parties with carnival atmospheres are held in the local Jewish communities. This festival celebrates the deliverance of the Persian Jews by Queen Esther and her Uncle Mordecai during the reign of King Ahasuerus (Xerxes) – 485-465 BC.

Full details of dates and venues of the above celebrations are available from the Central Enquiry Desk, Board of Deputies of British Jews on 01-387 4044.

JUDGES' SERVICE

The opening of the new legal year, usually on 1 October (or the first weekday in October if the date falls at the weekend), provides an opportunity for the public to see the dignitaries of the law in their full ceremonial robes. A Divine Service is held at approximately 1100 hrs in Westminster Abbey, attended by the various ranks of the judiciary, by Queen's Counsel, junior barristers and, in recent years, by distinguished guests invited from abroad, including members of the European Court. The service dates back to the Middle Ages and has its roots in the religious practice of the judges praying for guidance at the beginning of the legal term. Afterwards, the judges are entertained by the Lord Chancellor to a 'breakfast', held in the

Royal Gallery of the Houses of Parliament. The procession of the fully robed judges walk to Parliament across Old Palace Yard from the Abbey's Great West Door at 1145 hrs. The judges later return to the Royal Courts of Justice in the Strand and the new Law Year has then officially opened.

There is no public access to these ceremonies but the public can view the procession from Westminster Abbey to the Houses of Parliament.

On the day of the Service, a third tradition is carried out when, in the afternoon, the Lord Chancellor goes to the Law Courts in the Strand and presides in the court of the Lord Chief Justice of England and his own court. Here, at approximately 1345 hrs, there is another procession across the main hall of the Royal Courts of Justice, Strand, WC2.

A very limited number of tickets to view this short procession are available – apply in writing to The Superintendent, 10th Floor, Thomas More Building, Royal Courts of Justice, Strand, WC2A 2LL. Tel: 01-936 6208.

LORD CHANCELLOR

When acting as Speaker of the House of Lords the Lord Chancellor wears a black cloth court suit with a black silk gown and train, and a full-bottomed wig which were adopted by judges when they were the fashion in the 17th Century and have been worn ever since.

The Lord Chancellor's State Robes (shown here) are in black damask embroidered with gold lace. These are also worn by the Speaker and the Chancellor of the Exchequer and date back to the 16th century. They are worn at the opening of Parliament. The third ceremonial dress worn by the Lord Chancellor is an ordinary Peer's robe in velvet and ermine which he wears in the House together with a full-bottomed wig and tricorne hat for Royal Commissions.

KNOLLYS ROSE

Each summer in June a rose is presented to the Lord Mayor of London as a symbolic penalty imposed upon Lady Constance, wife of Sir Robert Knollys. In 1381 she built a bridge between two of her properties in Seething Lane, but forgot to get the Lord Mayor's permission. Possibly because of her position, only a nominal fine was made, in this case a rose. Such a fine or penalty was not unusual in those days and permission was granted on condition that a rose continued to be presented to the Lord Mayor each year. The ceremony fell into disuse after the Great Fire in 1666 when presumably the bridge was destroyed. In 1924 the ceremony was brought to life by the Rev. "Tubby" Clayton of Toc H fame, a Christian association which he established in the First World War. He arranged for a rose to be taken from the Port of London Authority's garden in Seething Lane and given to the Lord Mayor at Mansion House. This is the ceremony which continues today.

Only those personally invited by the company of Lightermen and Watermen attend this ceremony.

LION SERMON

This service is held on or near the 16 October at 1315 hrs in the church of St. Katharine Cree, 86 Leadenhall Street, EC3. It represents an expression of gratitude dating back three centuries and commemorates the miraculous escape of Sir John Gayer from a threatened attack by a lion. Each year the story is told in church. Sir John, a West Countryman came to London in 1620 to seek his fortune. He became a Sheriff of the City and prospered as a trader with the near East, particularly the Levant, which he periodically visited. On one of these trips through the desert he became separated from the main party. Eventually, completely exhausted, he fell asleep to be awakened in the middle of the night by the unmistakeable roar of a lion. Sir John closed his eyes and prayed and, as if nothing had happened, promptly fell asleep. When he was discovered in the morning by the main party, the imprints of a lion's paws were found on the ground where he had slept. Sir John returned to London and became Lord Mayor in 1647. But he never forgot his miraculous escape and made gifts to Christ's Hospital and various causes in Plymouth. He also made a bequest to the poor of the parish of St. Katharine Cree on condition that the story of his deliverance be told at a special service each year.

All visitors are welcome, no tickets required.

LILIES AND ROSES CEREMONY

On 21 May each year, a ceremony takes place at the Tower of London to honour the anniversary of the death of King Henry VI, founder of Eton College and King's College, Cambridge. Henry VI was believed to have been murdered in a small oratory in the Wakefield Tower in 1471 and it is on the spot where he was struck down that flowers are laid – white lilies from Eton College and white roses from King's College. Representatives of the colleges walk in procession from Queen's House at 1835 hrs with the

Resident Governor, Officers of the Tower, Yeoman Warders and the Chaplain of the Tower to this short service which commences at 1840 hrs.

The service is private and not open to the public.

LONDON TO BRIGHTON VETERAN CAR RUN

Always held on the first Sunday in November, this run attracts approximately 300 entrants. Enthusiasts from all over the world prime their veteran cars to take part in the gruelling run which leaves Hyde Park Corner between 0800 hrs and 0900 hrs to follow the main A23 road to Brighton, where they begin to arrive at approximately 1050 hrs.

The run began in 1896 when the law compelling motorists to have a man carrying a red flag walking in front of them was abolished. Motorists celebrated by destroying their flags and driving off to Brighton. The first organised run was in 1933 and only cars made between 1895 and 1905 can take part in the run today.

Arrive early to see the start at Hyde Park, or the finish at Madeira Drive, Brighton or stand anywhere along the route, to see the competitors.

RAC Motoring Services – 01-839 7050.

THE LONDON PRIVATE FIRE BRIGADES' COMPETITION

The London Private Fire Brigades Association comprises 66 Brigades. Since 1904 a competition, which chiefly involves target spraying by hoses, has been held in Guildhall Yard, EC2. Teams of six, mostly all volunteers, compete for a Silver Challenge Shield, which is presented by the City Corporation. A major penalty in the competition is the inadvertent spraying of competitors!

The competitions usually take place on a Saturday in May and September at approximately 1200 hrs. Spectators are welcome.

Information from the City of London on 01-606 3030.

LONDON RIDING HORSE PARADE

The London Riding Horse Parade was inaugurated in 1938 by the late Sir Walter Gilbey, a member of a famous equestrian family, who had been particularly active in attempting to maintain high standards of turnout and riding in London parks. The Parade is held annually in Rotten Row, Hyde Park, on the first Sunday in August. Commencing at 1400 hrs, Sir Walter Gilbey's original idea remains – to select the best turned out horse and rider. There are classes for Ladies Astride, Ladies Side Saddle, children, gentlemen and Riding Clubs or School Teams of three. The overall winner, the Supreme Champion, is awarded the much-coveted Moss Bros. perpetual Challenge Cup. Each entrant reaching a satisfying standard is given an Award of Merit Rosette.

Admission is free. Schedules and details of the event can be had from Brendan Byrne, Honorary Secretary, London Riding Horse Parade, 10a The Pavement, Chapel Road, West Norwood, SE27 0UN. Tel: 01-761 5651 evenings or weekends.

LORD MAYOR OF THE CITY OF LONDON

Election of Lord Mayor

The unbroken tradition of the City's mayoralty dates from 1192 when Henry Fitz Aylwyn became the first Mayor of London. All Aldermen who have served in the office of Sheriff, except past Lord Mayors, are in nomination for the election of Lord Mayor by the liverymen of the City companies and finally by the approbation of the Court of Aldermen. This ceremony, which is known as "Common Hall" takes place each year in Guildhall on or near St. Michaelmas Day (29 September). The reigning Lord Mayor and Sheriffs travel from Mansion House to Guildhall for the Election Ceremony at 1200 hrs. They are received by the Aldermen and Officers in the Livery Hall and are presented with nosegays of garden flowers by the Keeper of the Guildhall, a custom dating back to the days when sweet-scented flowers and herbs were regarded as protection against the infections and evil smells of the street.

Tickets for the ceremony are available free of charge from the Keeper of the Guildhall, Guildhall, EC2.

Before the Election takes place, a service is held at the Church of St. Lawrence Jewry, Gresham Street, EC2 at 1100 hrs. It is attended by the Lord Mayor, the Court of Aldermen, Officers and robed Masters of all the City Livery Companies, and dates back to the Election of Richard Whittington in 1406.

Visitors are welcome to attend.

Until the 18th century, the Lord Mayor had to hold office from his own house or from rented accommodation. This was remedied with the construction of an official residence, Mansion House, designed by George Dance the Elder (1739).

The new Lord Mayor has a year of exalted civic and social responsibility, during which he entertains visiting heads of state at banquets in Guildhall, (acting as a host secondary only to the Sovereign), represents the City abroad, attends in state the opening of the four annual sessions of the Central Criminal Court and makes perhaps 1,000 speeches.

The Lord Mayor's Procession

Since the Charter of King John in 1215 there has been a colourful procession to show the new Lord Mayor to the citizens of London on his way to swear allegiance to the Sovereign. From the 15th century until 1856 this procession went by barge to Westminster Hall. Since 1883 the Lord Mayor has taken his oath before the Monarch's Justices at the Royal Courts of Justice, which is on the route through Cheapside, Ludgate Hill and Fleet Street taken by the procession when it leaves Mansion House.

The Lord Mayor's Show as it is now known is usually held on the second Saturday in November starting at 1100 hrs and is a popular tradition, full of pomp and splendour.

The Lord Mayor travels in his gilded coach (normally in the Museum of London) drawn by six Shire horses and surrounded by his personal bodyguards composed of the Company of Pikemen and Musketeers of the Honourable Artillery Company.

The coach is preceded and followed by many floats which are finely decorated according to the theme chosen by the new Lord Mayor for that year. Also taking part are Naval, Regimental and Royal Air Force Bands.

Route-map from LTB or City of London Corporation.

Silent Ceremony

In years gone by the election of Lord Mayor was a fiercely contested battle which aroused tempers, frequently over-flowing into blood. Such was the degree of abuse hurled at contestants that the induction of a new Lord Mayor was often drowned by the protests of the unsuccessful candidates' supporters. Eventually, it was ruled that the change-over of the outgoing Lord Mayor for the new Lord Mayor should be held in complete silence. So it is that when the Lord Mayor is about to take office, (at 1500 hrs the day before the Lord Mayor's Procession) the symbols of his office, the Mace, the Crystal Sceptre, the Seal and the 16th century Privy Purse, are placed before him and the two mayors then exchange places without a word being said. The outgoing Lord Mayor is next seen only at the banquet held in his honour on the Monday following the Lord Mayors Show and thereafter retires into the shadows.

Tickets are available free in advance from: Keeper of Guildhall, Guildhall, EC2.

continued overleaf

PIKEMEN AND MUSKETEERS

Pikemen and musketeers of the Honourable Artillery Company. The pikemen and musketeers wear red tunics protected by metal breast and back plates, red knee britches, red stockings and soft moccasin style shoes. The pikemen wear a pointed protective helmet and the musketeers have a wide brimmed soft hat.

Election of Sheriffs

The Sheriff's office is the oldest of all City appointments, for the Shire-reeve, or Sheriff, existed as early as the 7th century. The office of Portreeve, named in the Charter of William the Conqueror, was the equivalent of Sheriff.

He has been elected by the Liverymen of the City since 1475. Since 1585 the election has always taken place on Midsummer's Day, or on a date as near as possible. Two Sheriffs are elected, and one, if not both, is expected to become a future Lord Mayor. The Sheriffs attend the Lord Mayor at most official functions and join in works of hospitality and charity. One of the Sheriffs attends throughout every day at the Central Criminal Court.

The ceremony, held in Guildhall at 1200 hrs is open to the general public. Apply in advance for tickets to the Keeper of Guildhall, Guildhall, London EC2.

THE LUTINE BELL

The Lutine Bell hangs above the rostrum in the centre of the vast new Underwriting Room at the new Lloyds Building in Lime Street, EC3. It is rung once for bad news and twice for good news. But it is no longer rung each time a ship is lost at sea. The bell came from the French frigate La Lutine taken by the British in 1793. The ship sank in a storm in 1799 and the bell was rescued in 1859, and installed at Lloyds in the old building. The bell was last rung on the 18 November 1986 when HM The Queen and HRH The Duke of Edinburgh officially opened the new Lloyds building.

The Lloyds Gallery is open to visitors and provides a view over the Underwriting Room, Mon-Fri 1000-1600 hrs.

MAUNDY MONEY

Maundy Money consists of specially-minted coins distributed annually on Maundy Thursday, (the Thursday before Easter) to as many men and as many women as the Sovereign has years. The origin of this tradition was the Last Supper when Jesus washed the Disciple's feet. It is the command (or Mandatum) of Jesus, to 'Do as I have done to you' that each Maundy ceremony is fulfilling, and the title is believed to derive from this word. The tradition of washing and kissing the feet of the recipients was last carried out by William III. The ceremony, dating back to the 12th century, is usually carried out by The Queen, or in her absence, by another member of the Royal Family or by the Lord High Almoner.

Recipients are always elderly but the qualification is no longer poverty; it is, instead a record of service to the Church and to the community. However, a qualification of hardship does apply to the Maundy children, two boys and two girls, usually orphans or children of a widowed mother. They walk in the procession, carrying nosegays, and receive the Maundy Money, a contribution also being made to the mother or guardian.

The ceremony is held in a different city each year and, although it was previously held at Westminster Abbey every fourth year, nowadays it is observed in provincial cities only. For venues, telephone LTB on 01-730 3488 nearer the date.

LONDON TOWN CRIER

The proclaimation of news by the town crier from the town hall steps was a common occurrence throughout Britain. Today's town criers perform ceremonial and promotional functions, wearing a uniform based on that of the Lord Mayor's.

LORD MAYOR'S CHAPLAIN

The Lord Mayor's Chaplain wears a "Geneva" gown of black over his cassock, preacher's tabs or bands around his collar and a scarf of black. Here he is shown as a former service chaplain and at the foot of each scarf are the service insignia; in this case of the Royal Navy. The Chaplain also carries a tricorne hat, wears buckled shoes, a black cummerbund and white gloves.

London has two independent police forces, the Metropolitan Police and the City Police; the latter covers the area of the City of London and "the Met" the rest of Greater London. The police became known as "bobbies" or "Peelers" from Sir Robert Peel, who as Home Secretary introduced the Metropolitan Police Act in 1829 which founded London's Police force. At first they tried to look as much like civilians as possible, wearing a top hat and short jacket with knee-length tails. Soon the top hat was replaced by a helmet. A variation of this is still worn by patrolling policemen today. The City police (who must all be over 5'11½" tall) wear a combed helmet emblazoned with the City crest, blue shirts as opposed to the white of the Metropolitan police, and red and white striped armlets and red checked cap bands (Policeman on the right). The first women police joined after the First World War; they wear a blue bowler hat with a check band with the emblem of the Met at the front matching that of the policeman's helmet. Traffic police and other car patrols wear flat caps – the helmet would not be very suitable!

MOSLEM FESTIVALS

The Central London Mosque at 146 Park Road, NW8 holds Moslem services at various times of the day throughout the week but the two festivals that attract Moslems from far and wide take place twice a year, dates according to the lunar calendar. They are the Festival of Idh-al-Fitr when prayers are said at the Mosque for the end of Ramadan (the month of fasting), and the second festival, Idh-al-Adha which takes place approximately two months later when prayers are said for the sacrifice of Abraham's son, Ishmael.

Visitors are welcome (including women) to bring along their prayer mats and join in. For dates, contact the Mosque on 01-724 3363.

NATIONAL SERVICE FOR SEAFARERS

Held on the Wednesday nearest 21 October, this service is closely aligned with Trafalgar Day (see p. 55). It is held in St. Paul's Cathedral at 1800 hrs, the burial place of Lord Nelson, and is dedicated to all those who have spent a life-time at sea either in the Royal Navy, the Merchant Navy, a fishing fleet, or as a pilot light-house keeper, and lifeboatman. It was inaugurated in 1905, the centenary of the Battle of Trafalgar. The Choir is provided by naval schools and special prayers, including that used by the Royal Navy, are said. The colours of the nautical schools are received at the high altar. This is one of the few occasions in London at which the band of the Royal Marines can be seen. They play in the North Transept of the Cathedral before and after the service.

Admission is by ticket, free of charge on prior application to be received not later than 12 September from: The Hon. Secretary, Annual National Service for Seafarers, St. Michael Paternoster Royal, College Hill, EC4R 2RL.

NEW YEAR'S EVE

It is customary to hold parties all over London on New Year's Eve, 31 December when, on the stroke of midnight, everyone joins hands and sings "Auld Lang Syne", a traditional song taken from a poem by the great 18th century Scots poet, Burns. A well established tradition is the celebration which takes place in Trafalgar Square when thousands of people gather in festive mood to bring in the New Year – previously accompanied by high-spirited dancing in the fountains! These are now boarded up for the occasion. Parliament Square is another popular location for watching Big Ben strike 12 on New Year's Eve.

NOTTING HILL CARNIVAL

The Notting Hill Carnival has become a popular West Indian event among Londoners and visitors, since it was originally conceived in 1965 as a children's carnival. Carnival-goers dance and sing together in the streets around Notting Hill and Ladbroke Grove, W8 to the music of steel bands, brass bands, soca sounds and spectacular costume dances. Other attractions are floats, outdoor discotheques, limbo dancing and stalls selling West Indian food. The Carnival is always held on August Bank

continued overleaf

PEARLY KINGS & QUEENS

"Pearlies" are traditionally costermongers, (street traders), each borough or street market having once had a Coster King and his wife as the Coster Queen. They were originally elected to safeguard the costermongers' rights from competitors and roughs; these bodies were, in fact, early forms of trade unions and they existed in this form until street licensing was introduced. There is some debate as to how the "Pearlies" costume originated. Some say that the coster comedian Albert Chevalier (1851-1923), sang "The Coster's Serenade" whilst dressed in a coster costume decorated with pearl buttons. Others say the costumes were a "take-off" of the clothes worn by the early Edwardian dandies. Another theory is the early French vegetable sellers who traded in the streets of London and who decorated their coats with sequins. The original Pearly King was Henry Croft who appeared in a suit encrusted with pearl buttons in about 1880. He is buried in St. Pancras Cemetery, N2 and an effigy of him in top hat and Pearly suit stands above his grave.

The typical Pearly costume is a jacket with large lapels and two or four large pockets, often a long waistcoat, bell-bottomed trousers and for headgear, a plush skull or cloth cap – all covered in pearl buttons. A colourful silk neckerchief is normally added. For the women, velvet skirts studded with buttons and magnificent Gainsborough hats adorned with ostrich feathers that have been dyed and curled, are worn. The Pearlies have their own hierachy; their children are known as pearly princes and princesses and are christened in regal manner in pearly-studded gowns that have been handed down through the generations.

Henry Croft started collecting for Dr. Barnado's in his local borough of Summertown (now known as St. Pancras, Kings Cross) and as the Pearly "family" grew, so did this practice of collecting for local charities.

Today, Pearly Kings and Queens can be seen at many events such as the Lord Mayor's Show, The Easter Parade, the Pearly Harvest Festival and at London's street markets, particularly Petticoat Lane.

Holiday Sunday and Monday and continues into the early hours. The Children's Carnival is the main attraction on Sunday and includes a competition for the best costume for which judging takes place at 1500 hrs. There is also a competition for best costume held for adults on the Monday and judging takes place at 1500 hrs on this day.

Details and information are available from the Carnival Arts Committee on 01-960 5266.

ORANGES AND LEMONS SERVICE

On the third or fourth Thursday in March, the children of St. Clement Danes Primary School in Drury Lane visit the Church of St. Clement Danes, Strand, WC2 for a short afternoon service, starting at 1500 hrs with the tune of the rhyme "Oranges and Lemons, say the bells of St. Clement's". After the service each child is given an orange and a lemon.

This charming annual ceremony was first started by the Rev. W. Pennington Bickford in 1920 (who was then vicar of the Parish) when a carillon was installed so the ancient bells would ring out the old nursery rhyme. The re-cast bells ring out the old rhyme at 0900, 1200, 1500 and 1800 hrs daily.

All visitors are welcome, no tickets required.

PANCAKE DAY

Shrove Tuesday, the day before Ash Wednesday in February or March marks the beginning of Lent and is the day on which people were expected to 'shrive' (confess) their sins before Lent. The original idea of eating pancakes was to use up all the meat, butter and eggs which could not be eaten in Lent. Shrove Tuesday has always involved boisterous celebrations. All over the country pancake races are still held in which contests are run with a frying pan, at the same time tossing the pancakes in the air. London venues have changed over the years, at present there are races at Covent Garden, held every Shrove Tuesday, in which anyone can take part. They take place from midday and are followed by a band performance.

Alternative Arts 01-240 5451.

At Westminster School, behind closed doors, the ceremony of Pancake Greaze takes place in the School Hall. This custom is several hundred years old and involves the school chef in cooking a massive pancake which is carried into Hall where it is tossed over a high bar. The boys fight for the pieces and the boy who has collected the largest piece (each piece is weighed) collects a golden guinea.

Private ceremony – no public admitted.

PEARLY HARVEST FESTIVAL SERVICE

Pearly Kings and Queens are traditionally cockney costermongers and the best occasion to see them is at the Pearly Harvest Festival – a service held at 1500 hrs on the first Sunday in October at the Church of St. Martin-in-the-Fields, WC2. The altar and the pulpit are arrayed with the fruits of the

continued overleaf

earth, a Pearly King reads one of the Lessons and the congregation sings the hymns of the harvest season.

London's costermongers, with their barrows and stalls of fruit and vegetables, have been part of the London scene as far back as mediaeval times, but their famous costumes only came into being during the last two decades of the 19th century.

Members of the public are welcome to attend the service.

THE PEPYS COMMEMORATION SERVICE

The Pepys Commemoration service is held at 1200 hrs in St. Olave's Church, Hart Street, EC3 towards the end of May. St. Olave's was the official Church of Samuel Pepys in his position as a senior administrator of the Navy Office and a special pew was reserved for him as Clerk of the Acts to the Navy. It was later that he became Secretary of the Admiralty and still retained the pew. On the death of his wife, Elizabeth, whom he loved greatly, he had a monument erected in the Church and when he died some 30 years later, he was buried in the same vault as that of Elizabeth. A memorial service is held once a year at which the Lord Mayor places a wreath in front of the memorial as a tribute to London's greatest diarist. Music of the 17th century is played and the lesson is given by a noted Pepys authority.

Members of the public are welcome to attend the service. No tickets are necessary but it is best to arrive early. A buffet lunch with a glass of wine is available after the service at a small cost. It is advisable to book for this by writing to the church at least a week in advance.

PUNCH AND JUDY FESTIVALS

On 9 May 1662, Samuel Pepys reputedly watched the first Punch and Judy Show to take place in England, under the portico of St. Paul's Church in Covent Garden. It is therefore appropriate that Covent Garden should host two Punch and Judy Festivals.

The first Punch and Judy Festival normally takes place every second Sunday in May. There is a procession round Covent Garden at approximately 1000 hrs and a church service at 1100 hrs. Punch and Judy performances take place in the church garden from 1200 hrs until 1800 hrs.

All are welcome to attend. No charge is made to watch the shows although performers do take collections. Information: Actor's Church Union – 01-836 5221.

The Punch and Judy Fellowship also hold a festival in Covent Garden, on the Piazza either on the last Sunday in September or the first Sunday in October. This attracts a bevy of Punch and Judy Shows from all over the country as well as guests from Europe. Performances continue throughout the day.

Information: Professor Percy Press II – 01-802 4656.

QUIT RENT CEREMONY

Every October the Comptroller of the City Corporation performs a ceremony at the Law Courts in front of the Queen's Remembrancer to pay a quit-rent for two holdings, the Moors in Shropshire and the Forge in St. Clement Danes, in a custom which goes back to the 13th century. For the Shropshire property, where the area is uncertain today, the Comptroller presented two knives, one sharp enough to cut a hazel stick with one blow, the other so weak that it would "bend in new cheese." These knives have been replaced by a billhook and hatchet which are annually presented by the Comptroller who is also the City Solicitor to the Queen's Remembrancer. The Forge property is settled by a payment of six horse-shoes and 61 nails. This originates from the jousting tournaments held on the adjoining land which involved the replacement of one of the Knight's horse-shoes.

This ceremony is open to the public – write in advance to: The Master Secretary's Office, Room 118, Royal Courts of Justice, London WC2. Tel: 01-936 6000.

TRADITIONAL PUPPETMEN

The Punch and Judy Show first came to England in 1662 as a marionnette show with the Italian travelling troupe, Comedia dell Arte. The show, as we know it today, developed in the 19th century when Punch and Judy glove puppet booths appeared at fairs throughout the country. There is never one set script although each show normally includes the central characters, Punch, his wife Judy, their baby, the policeman and the butcher and relies on improvisation and audience participation.

The "Professor" operates the puppets and his helper is known as the Bottler. The Bottler plays music on instruments such as drums or bugle, to attract people's attention, encourages the audience to participate in the show and takes collections afterwards. The Professor has always dressed flamboyantly and even today he can be seen in gaily coloured trousers – often striped or checked and brightly coloured top hat and tails. He places a "swazzle" (a small instrument made of tin and fabric) at the back of his mouth and this changes his voice into that of the characteristic puppets.

RED FEATHER DAY – SIR JOHN CASS

Sir John Cass was born on 20 February 1661 in East Smithfield and became a noted educationalist. The service to his memory, known as Red Feather Day, is held at approximately 1130 hrs on the nearest Friday to that date, in the Church of St.Botolph Without Aldgate, Aldgate High Street, EC3, near the site where he founded his school. John Cass prospered in the City and was the master of two livery companies. He was also an Alderman and Sheriff of the City and became its Member of Parliament. His principal ambition, however, was to found a school bearing his name and in 1710 he built his school within the churchyard of St. Botolph. In 1718, as he lay dying, his great concern was that his wife should have a sufficiently large endowment to maintain the school. With a quill pen in hand, he was about to sign the necessary paper to ensure this when he had a pulmonary haemorrhage and the pen became bloodstained. Today, a scarlet plume (a turkey quill dyed red) is used to symbolise his memory and is worn in the hats or the lapels of the children from the John Cass School who attend the ceremony in memory of his blood-stained pen. After the service the Governors of the Sir John Cass Foundation and masters of the school drink a loving cup of hot mulled wine made from a recipe which dates back to his time.

Public welcome to attend the service but must arrive early. Contact the church nearer the time for date: 01-283 1670

REMEMBRANCE SUNDAY

A memorial day for all three services and Allied Forces who gave their lives in the two World Wars, takes place on the second Sunday in November.

Detachments of the Armed Forces and ex-servicemen and women assemble at the Cenotaph Memorial in Whitehall, SW1 and band music is played while awaiting the arrival of HM The Queen at 1059 hrs. A two-minute silence at 1100 hrs is heralded and ended by a gun fired from Horse Guards Parade, after which the Last Post is sounded by Buglers of the Royal Marines. The Queen then lays a wreath at the Cenotaph, followed by members of the Royal Family, representatives of the Government, Commonwealth Governments and the Services. The Bishop of London conducts a short service of Remembrance with a Blessing, Reveille and the National Anthem.

On the previous day, the Royal Albert Hall plays host to the Royal British Legion Festival of Remembrance with two performances, one at 1430 hrs, the other at 1930 hrs. Priority for tickets is given to members of the Legion, but a few are available to the general public for the afternoon performance, from mid-September.

Contact: Box Office, Royal Albert Hall, Kensington Gore, London SW7. Tel: 01-589 8212.

ROAD SWEEPING BY THE VINTNERS' COMPANY

Members of the Vintners' Company fulfil an annual ruling laid down many centuries ago that on Installation Day (normally the second Wednesday in July) the Company's "tackle porters" – wine porters – "shall sweep the road with full besom" between the Vintners' Hall, Upper Thames Street and their church of St. James, Garlickhythe, EC4, in order that the Master, Warden, and Brethren of the Court of Assistants step not in the foulness or litter of our streets and further that each Master, Warden or Brother of the Court of Assistants be provided with a nosegay of sweet and fine herbs that their nostrils be not offended by any noxious flavours or other ill vapours".

So it is today that members of the company walk in procession at 1150 hrs from their hall to the Church with the master and Wardens carrying their nosegays and preceded by a "tackle porter" sweeping the road ahead of them. The procession returns from the Church to Vintners' Hall at about 1240 hrs.

Visitors may watch the procession, which takes ten minutes. Limited space is available in the church for the service – no tickets are required.

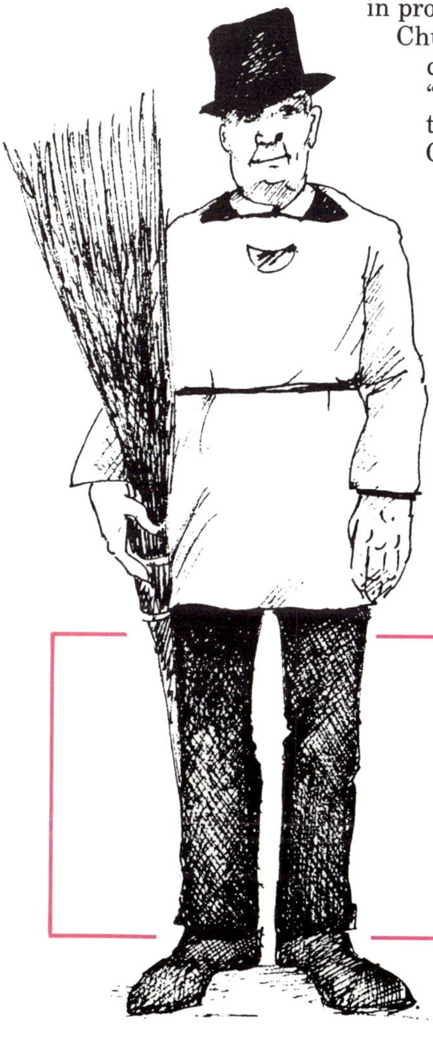

WINE PORTER

The Wine Porter (also known as the Wine Tackle Porter) is employed by the Vintners Livery Company. He dons a top hat for ceremonial occasions and wears a white smock, or dress.

ROYAL ASCOT

Royal Ascot is held on the Tuesday to Friday of the third week in June. The first race meeting at the Berkshire course was inaugurated by Queen Anne in 1711 – while following the Royal Buckhounds through nearby Windsor Forest, she decided Ascot Heath would be a suitable spot for horse racing.

Ascot attracts the cream of 'Society', especially on Thursday, the famous "Gold Cup" Day (also known as "Ladies Day" when many weird and wonderful hats are worn). It is attended by The Queen and the Royal Family who drive from Windsor each day in open carriages. The Royal Procession goes down the course at 1400 hrs, before the first race at 1430 hrs.

Applications for admission to the Royal Enclosure should be made in writing between January and March to: Her Majesty's Representative, Ascot Office, St. James's Palace, SW1A 1BP. (The signature of a sponsor is required.)

Overseas visitors should apply to their Ambassador or High Commissioner, or through the Commonwealth Office in London. Those attending in the Royal Enclosure must wear formal dress and top hats. Other tickets are available in advance from: The Secretary, Grand Stand, Ascot, Berkshire. Tel: Ascot (0990) 22211.

THE ROYAL TOURNAMENT

The Royal Tournament, one of Britain's greatest traditions and first held in 1880 at the Agricultural Halls, Islington, (then known as the Grand Military Tournament and Assault-at-Arms), is a 2½ hour action-packed spectacular presented by the Armed Forces in aid of Service Charities. Always held for two and a half weeks in mid-July at Earls Court, the programme combines pomp, colour, pageantry and excitement, appealing to all ages.

Some of the Tournament's traditional attractions are legendary: The Musical Drive of the King's Troop, Royal Horse Artillery, which has been bringing dash, colour and brilliant horsemanship to the Royal Tournament since 1896, and the Royal Navy Field Gun Race in which elite teams from Portsmouth, Devonport and Fleet Air Arm compete. HM The Queen and other senior members of the Royal Family are patrons of the Royal Tournament and attend performances to take the Salute.

Tickets are available from the middle of March from the Royal Tournament Box Office, Earls Court Exhibition Centre, Warwick Road, SW5 9TA. Tel: 01-373 8141.

The Tournament is preceded by a preview parade – the Mall March – on the Sunday before the show opens although this does not always take place in London.

SILENT CEREMONY

See 'The Lord Mayor' (p. 37).

SPEAKER'S CORNER

In 1855, 150,000 people gathered in the north-east corner of Hyde Park to demonstrate against Lord Robert Grosvenor's Sunday Trading Bill. At that time, there was no legal right of assembly there and the police arrived to arrest an agitator but he had already gone. After more demonstrations, the right of assembly was recognised in 1872 and this part of the park became known as Speaker's Corner.

Anyone may orate on any subject, provided the speech is not obscene or blasphemous, or does not constitute an incitement to a breach of the peace. Extraordinary public speeches and conversations may be heard each day, although the most popular day is Sunday – late morning or early afternoon.

SPITAL SERMON

This service which is held in the Guild Church of St. Lawrence Jewry-next-Guildhall, EC2, at 1200 hrs on the first Thursday after Easter, takes its name from the Hospital of St. Mary Spital which was founded in 1197 by Walter Brown and Rose, his wife. It was closed in 1538 and Spital Square now marks the site. In the churchyard was an outdoor pulpit called the Spital Cross where sermons were preached at Easter to the Lord Mayor, Aldermen and others. The sermons continued after the hospital's closure and although they were stopped during the Commonwealth, they were revived at the Restoration, taking place at various city churches. From 1707 to 1940, the sermon was preached at Christchurch, Newgate Street but since that church was bombed in the Second World War St. Lawrence Jewry has been the venue. The Lord Mayor, Sheriffs and Aldermen of the City of London attend the service after a colourful procession from Guildhall, across the yard to the Church.

All visitors are welcome, no tickets required.

ST. KATHARINE'S DAY

St. Katharine was martyred on the wheel in about AD 307 in Alexandria by order of the Roman Emperor Maximilian because of her refusal to renounce the Christian faith. A Hospice and Chapel of "St. Katharine by the Tower" was built and endowed to care for the sick and poor by Queen Matilda in 1148. This site has now become the London World Trade Centre in St. Katharine Docks. Each year on 25 November, the Saint's feast day, it was a custom for money to be given out to the ancient Hospice for the local poor. The custom is continued to this day with newly minted coins being distributed to children from local schools after a short service held at the Coronarium which marks the site of the original Chapel of St. Katharine.

Spectators welcome.

STATE OPENING OF PARLIAMENT

This ceremony is usually held in late October or early November (or at another time of year if a new government has come to power at an election). Held at the House of Lords, Westminster, the ceremony itself is not open to the general public. Before HM The Queen arrives, her bodyguard of Yeomen of the Guard search the cellars of the Palace of Westminster (see p. 27).

The Queen and the Duke of Edinburgh travel in the Irish State Coach

THE SPEAKER OF THE HOUSE OF COMMONS

On normal sitting days the Speaker wears a black cloth court suit with linen bands over which is worn a black silk robe with train. He also wears a full-bottomed wig and carries a tricorne hat. On state occasions such as the Opening of Parliament he wears a splendid robe of black satin damask trimmed with gold and at the neck a lace jabot and lace frills at the sleeves. (The latter is illustrated).

from Buckingham Palace, leaving at approximately 1100 hrs. The procession moves down the Mall and through Horse Guards Parade to Whitehall and stops by the Lords entrance of the Houses of Parliament. The Imperial State Crown precedes the Queen from the Palace in its own carriage at 1037 hrs. A Gun Salute is fired at Hyde Park at 1115 hrs, (1200 hrs at the Tower of London) (see p. 28), as the Queen enters the House of Lords, walking in procession to the throne in the Chamber. When the Queen has taken her place upon the throne the moment comes for the entry of the Commons. The Lord Great Chamberlain raises his wand, which is the sign that he has received the Queen's command for the Commons to be summoned, and the Queen's Messenger, the Gentleman Usher of the Black Rod, sets out for the door which leads to the Commons. Here a traditional ritual takes place which serves as a reminder of the abuse of royal privilege in the attempted arrest of Five Members in 1642 by Charles I, which was a major contributory factor to the Civil War. As Black Rod approaches the door the Serjeant at Arms slams it shut whereupon Black Rod knocks three times upon the door with his rod. The Serjeant at Arms opens the grille, peers through and the Queen's Messenger requests admittance. On this request being granted by the Speaker, the Serjeant at Arms opens the door and Black Rod enters to convey his message; then members of the Commons, led by the Speaker, and the Serjeant at Arms bearing the Mace, proceed to the House of Lords. On arrival of the Commons at the Bar of the House of Lords, the Queen reads the "Most Gracious Speech", giving the elected Government's policies and programme for the coming session of Parliament.

Telephone 01-219 4272 (in the autumn) for exact date.

STOW COMMEMORATION

Once a year on a day in April at 1200 hrs, a service of commemoration for John Stow (1525-1605) is held in the Church of St. Andrew Undershaft, Leadenhall Street, EC3. John Stow was a master tailor and a historian, and his love of history was his downfall. He became a master tailor at the relatively young age of 24 and carried out his trade with great proficiency for 15 years. But history and historical research dominated his life. For six days every week, John Stow would sit at his desk, quill pen in hand laboriously making copious notes and producing learned historical documents. His survey of London is still valued by historians today. He paid no attention to his business whatsoever and ran out of money. King James I heard of Stow and his work and the predicament he faced, and allowed him to become a licensed beggar in order that he could continue his work. There is a statue of John Stow depicting him with a quill in his hand and a look of deep meditation in St. Andrew Undershaft and once a year in his memory an address is given by a distinguished historian. At the same time the quill in the effigy's hand is replaced by a new one.

Public welcome to attend, no tickets required.

SWAN MARKER OF THE VINTNERS' COMPANY

At the time of writing, the Vintners' Company's Swan Marker and Bargemaster is Mr Bill Colley. This ancient river appointment has strong hereditary links and skills and his duties are extensive, covering the stretch of river from Windsor to the sea. He is responsible for the swans at all hours and tasks include removing fishhooks and fishing tackle from swans and the rescue of injured or stray birds – this can sometimes be a swan which has flown and crashlanded on a busy road or railway line.

Mr Colley has two costumes which he wears when he is involved in two major ceremonies which take place during the year. The first is Swan Upping when he wears a green blazer with silver trim, white trousers and a naval cap with swan feathers. The second is the Road Sweeping Ceremony in July when he wears a black and silver Elizabethan frock coat which has a large silver badge on the left sleeve. The latter costume is also worn at ceremonial occasions which take place at Vintners' Hall.

SWAN UPPING

The traditional ceremony of Swan Upping on the River Thames, believed to have been held for over 300 years, normally takes place during the third week of July. As long as records exist, swans have been regarded as royal birds, although ownership of swans on the River Thames is vested in HM The Queen, the Vintners' Company and the Dyers' Company – two of the ancient Livery companies of the City of London.

Starting at Sunbury-on-Thames six skiffs pull up river together to Whitchurch. They catch all the swan families on the Thames and record the numbers. The Queen's birds remain unmarked but the other cygnets are marked with nicks on their beaks, according to their ownership. The Vintners' birds are given two nicks and the Dyers' birds one.

The boats start at different points each day, contact 01-236 1863 for details.

SWEARING ON THE HORNS

Swearing on the Horns in Highgate is and always has been an informal custom, but it used to be one in which most London-bound stage coach travellers from the North were expected to participate.

In 1826 there were 19 taverns in Highgate and most of them kept a pair of horns for use in the ceremony – either ram's or stag's horns. As soon as the "unsworn" travellers had been detected, the landlord of the inn, would don wig and black gown, then accompanied by a "Clerk", who carried a pole with the horns attached, the swearing would commence.

The version used today (published in 1796) is as follows:

"Pray, Sir, lay your Right Hand on this Book, and attend to the Oath. You swear by the Rules of Sound Judgement that you will not eat Brown Bread when you can have White, except you like the Brown the better; that you will not drink Small Beer when you can get Strong, except you like the Small Beer better; but you will kiss the Maid in preference to the Mistress, if you like the Maid better – so help you Billy Bodkin – Turn around and fulfil your Oath."

Following the Oath, the candidate is declared a "Freeman of Highgate" as follows:

"If at any time you are going through Highgate and want to rest yourself, and you see a pig lying in a ditch you have liberty to kick her out and take her place; but if you see three lying together you must only kick out the middle one and lie between the other two."

The ceremony is still carried out on an evening in Spring and Autumn at Ye Olde Wrestlers Tavern, North Road, N6 and an evening in July at the Red Lion & Sun, North Road, N6 (these venues may change). Visitors can "swear an oath" in front of the "Judge" and become "Freemen of Highgate" (a small charge is made for the certificates) and a yard of ale contest is also held.

The ceremony, in aid of the Hornsey Trust for Handicapped Children, takes place from 2030-2400 hrs. For dates, telephone 01-340 1846.

BLACK ROD

Black Rod, an officer of the Houses of Parliament, wears a court dress – black shoes, silk stockings, black breeches and a black coat. On ceremonial occasions he wears ruffles at the wrist and a jabot at the neck as shown here. The Rod, which was first mentioned in the 14th century, is carried on ceremonial occasions such as the State Opening of Parliament. It is made of ebony with a gold lion at the top. Black Rod's chain of office carries a gold knot surrounded by the garter, and surmounted by the Crown. Black Rod also takes part in Garter ceremonies wearing the scarlet mantle of an Officer of the Order of the Garter with his chain of office and the Black Rod.

TRAFALGAR DAY PARADE (Royal Naval Association)

The Royal Naval Association hold their reunion for all members every two years at the Royal Albert Hall on a Saturday evening as near to Trafalgar Day (21 October) as possible followed by the Parade and Service of Remembrance at the Cenotaph on the Sunday at 1100 hrs. The Parade forms up on Horse Guards Parade and marches to the Cenotaph at 1100 hrs for a special remembrance service for all naval people who have given their lives for the country over the centuries. Wreaths are laid by the Area representatives of the Association from all over the United Kingdom, and the President of the Association lays a wreath in the form of an anchor made of poppies by war-disabled veterans at the Royal British Legion Poppy Factory. After the service, the Parade returns to Horse Guards Parade with Standards flying behind the Royal Marines Bands for the march past.

Spectators are welcome. Information from the Royal Naval Association and Headquarters 01-352 6764.

TRAFALGAR DAY PARADE Sea Cadets

This has moved to Portsmouth but may return to London in 1989, contact LTB for information.

TRIAL OF THE PYX

The Trial of the Pyx is a regular, independent check on the accuracy of composition and weight of the coins of the realm and has been carried out since the days of Henry III. The Trial is held in February or March at Goldsmiths' Hall, Foster Lane, EC2 and is presided over by the Queen's Remembrancer. It is handled by a chosen jury of "discreet" men, Freemen of the Goldsmiths' Company and many of them leaders of the financial world of the City of London.

The Pyx (meaning boxes), contain coins in sealed bags, which each hold 50 coins. These coins have been put aside throughout the past year by the Mint Foremen who are responsible for taking one coin from every batch minted. After swearing an oath, each member of the Jury takes a coin from each bag and places it in a copper bowl before him. The remaining 49 in each bag are put into a wooden bowl and so the process is repeated. The coins in each Jury members copper bowl are taken for assay which takes some eight weeks. The Trial is then reconvened in May when the Queen's Remembrancer returns to Goldsmiths' Hall to ask the Jury for their verdict. Once the verdict has been given the Jury and guests retire to the Livery Hall for the Pyx Luncheon, at which the Chancellor of the Exchequer, as Master of the Mint, is always the principal speaker. The Pyx Luncheon brings the Trial of the Pyx to a close.

This ceremony is not open to the public.

TROOPING THE COLOUR

Trooping the Colour celebrates the Sovereign's official birthday and usually takes place on the second Saturday in June. It was in 1805 that the ceremony first took its present form although the parade does originate from much earlier times when it had a practical purpose – the display of the regimental colour (flag) to the fighting men so that they would be familiar with it as a rallying point on the battlefield.

The Queen, wearing the uniform of the Foot Guards whose colour is being trooped, and the Sovereign's Escort of the Household Cavalry leave Buckingham Palace at approximately 1040 hrs and go down The Mall to Horse Guards arriving at 1100 hrs. As the Queen reaches the Saluting Base the National Anthem is played and a Gun Salute is fired in Hyde Park (see p.28). She then inspects the parade and on returning to the Saluting Base, the whole spectacle of the Birthday Parade unfolds. As it draws to a close, each regiment passes before the Queen. The Queen proceeding in front of her Foot Guards arrives back at Buckingham Palace at 1230 hrs and appears on the balcony for a flypast by the RAF at 1300 hrs. There is also another gun salute at 1300 hrs at the Tower of London. From 1987 the Queen will attend this ceremony in a carriage and not on horseback.

Tickets are allocated by ballot and are limited to two per application. If you are unsuccessful in the ballot for the ceremony itself, your application, if you wish, may be included in the ballots for tickets for the rehearsals on the two Saturdays preceding the ceremony (please state this on your application). Written application for tickets should be made to the following address before 1 March: The Brigade Major (Trooping the Colour), Headquarters, Household Division, Horse Guards, Whitehall, SW1A 2AX.

TYBURN WALK

On the last Sunday in April each year, at approximately 1500 hrs, a Catholic Bishop leads a silent procession of up to 500 people from the Old Bailey to Tyburn Convent, 8 Hyde Park Place, Bayswater Road, W2 (between Stanhope Place and Hyde Park Street). The procession, followed by a service at 1700 hrs, is in memory of those Catholics martyred for their faith during the 16th and 17th centuries at the nearby Tyburn Gallows, and follows the exact route that was taken from Newgate Prison to Tyburn.

The approximate site of the triangular gallows is marked by a stone in the traffic island at the junction of Edgware Road and Bayswater Road.

Public welcome to attend. Information from Monsignor A. Stark on 01-947 2598.

VINTAGE FESTIVAL SERVICE

St. Olave's Church, Hart Street, EC3 is the Parish Church of the Wine and Spirit Trade of London. Each year, a vintage festival service is held here at 1200 hrs on the first Tuesday in October. It is attended by the Masters and Wardens of the Worshipful Companies of Vintners and Distillers who arrive in full regalia to celebrate the year's successful wine harvest.

Members of the general public are welcome to attend the service and the buffet lunch and wine (there is a small charge for this) which is served in the Church after the service. No tickets are required.

TRADITIONAL EVENTS MONTH BY MONTH

An up to date list is available free from LTB; published in January each year. Additional information from the London Tourist Board on 01-730 3488.

JANUARY

Baddeley Cake
Theatre Royal, Drury Lane, WC2

Charles I Commemoration
Banqueting House, Whitehall, SW1

Epiphany Gifts
Chapel Royal, St. James's Palace, SW1

FEBRUARY

Blessing the Throats
St. Etheldreda's Church, Ely Place, EC1

Chinese New Year

Clown's Service
Holy Trinity Church, Dalston, E8

Gun Salute – Accession Day

Pancake Day Races
Covent Garden, WC2

Trial of the Pyx
Goldsmiths' Company Hall, Foster Lane, EC2

MARCH

Head of the River Race
Mortlake to Putney

Jewish Festival – Purim, Feast of Lots

Oranges and Lemons Service
St. Clement Danes, Strand, WC2

Oxford v Cambridge University Boat Race
Putney to Mortlake

Spring Equinox
Tower Hill Terrace, EC3

APRIL

Butterworth Charity
St. Bartholomew the Great, Smithfield, EC1

Easter Parade
Battersea Park, SW11

Gun Salute – Queen's Birthday

Hot Cross Bun Ceremony
Widow's Son Inn, 75 Devons Road, E3

London Harness Horse Parade
Regent's Park, NW1

Maundy Money

Spital Sermon
St. Lawrence Jewry, EC2

Stow Commemoration
St. Andrew Undershaft, EC3

Tyburn Walk
Old Bailey to Tyburn Convent

MAY

Beating the Bounds
All Hallows by the Tower, EC3
St. Peter Ad Vincula, EC3

Chelsea Flower Show
Royal Hospital, SW3

Dunkirk Veterans Service
St. Lawrence Jewry, EC2

Historic Commercial Vehicle Run
Battersea Park to Brighton

Idh-al-Fitr
Central London Mosque, 146 Park Road, NW8

Israel Independence Day

Lilies & Roses Ceremony
Tower of London, EC3

London Private Fire Brigades Competition – Challenge Shield
Guildhall Yard, EC2

Punch 325th Anniversary Celebrations
Covent Garden Piazza, WC2

Swearing on the Horns
Ye Olde Wrestlers' Tavern, N6

JUNE

Beating Retreat – Household Division
Horse Guards Parade, SW1

Bubble Sermon
St. Martin's-within-Ludgate, EC4

Derby Day
Epsom Racecourse, Surrey

Election of Sheriffs
Guildhall, EC2

Garter Service
St. George's Chapel, Windsor

Gun Salute – Duke of Edinburgh's Birthday

Founder's Day
Royal Hospital, SW3

Knollys Rose
Mansion House, EC2

Pepys Commemoration Service
St. Olave's Church, Hart Street, EC3

Royal Ascot
Ascot Racecourse, Berks.

Sounding Retreat
Horse Guards Parade, SW1 (Light Division)

Trooping the Colour
Horse Guards Parade, SW1

JULY

Cart Marking
Guildhall Yard, EC2

Doggett's Coat & Badge Race
London Bridge to Chelsea

Henley Royal Regatta
Henley-on-Thames, Oxfordshire

Henry Wood Promenade Concerts
Royal Albert Hall, SW7

Road Sweeping by the Vintners' Company
Vintners' Hall to St. James Garlickhythe

Royal Tournament
Earls Court Centre, SW5

Sanskritik Festival of the Arts of India
South Bank, SE1

Swan Upping
Sunbury-on-Thames to Whitchurch

Swearing on the Horns
Red Lion & Sun, North Road, N6

AUGUST

Gun Salute – Queen Mother's Birthday

Idh-al-Adha
Central London Mosque, 146 Park Road, NW8

London Riding Horse Parade
Rotten Row, Hyde Park, W2

Notting Hill Carnival
Notting Hill & Ladbroke Grove, W8

continued overleaf

SEPTEMBER

Autumn Equinox
Primrose Hill, Regent's Park, NW3

Christ's Hospital Service
St. Sepulchre, High Holborn, WC1

Clog and Apron Race
Kew Gardens, Richmond, Surrey

Cromwell's Day
Oliver Cromwell Statue, Cromwell Green, SW1

Election of Lord Mayor
Guildhall, EC2

Farthing Bundles
Leadenham Court, Spanby Road, E3

Horseman's Sunday
St. John & St. Michael, Hyde Park Crescent, W2

Trafalgar Day Parade – Royal Naval Association
Cenotaph, Whitehall, SW1

OCTOBER

Diwali, Festival of Lights

Harvest of the Sea Thanksgiving Service
St. Mary-at-Hill, Lovat Lane, EC3

Judges' Service
Westminster Abbey, SW1

Lion Sermon
St. Katharine Cree Church, EC3

London Private Fire Brigades Competition – UK Championships
Guildhall Yard, EC2

National Service for Seafarers
St. Paul's Cathedral, EC4

Pearly Harvest Festival
St. Martin-in-the-Fields, WC2

Punch & Judy Festival
Covent Garden Piazza, WC2

Quit Rent Ceremony
Royal Courts of Justice, WC2

State Opening of Parliament
House of Lords, SW1

Vintage Festival
St. Olave's Church, Hart Street, EC3

NOVEMBER

Christmas Lights
Regent Street and Oxford Street

Fireworks Night

London to Brighton Veteran Car Run
Hyde Park Corner to Madeira Drive

Lord Mayor's Show
City of London

Remembrance Sunday Ceremony
Cenotaph, SW1

St. Katharine's Day
Coronarium, St. Katharine Docks

Silent Ceremony
Guildhall, EC2

DECEMBER

Boar's Head Presentation
Mansion House, EC2

Christmas Tree
Trafalgar Square, WC2

INDEX